·THE·
PEOPLE'S PALACE
and
GLASGOW GREEN

D1323919

· THE ·
PEOPLE'S PALACE
ℰand℔
GLASGOW GREEN

Elspeth King

Chambers

First published 1985 by Richard Drew Publishing Ltd
Second edition 1988

This edition published 1991 by W & R Chambers Ltd,
43–45 Annandale Street, Edinburgh EH7 4AZ

Reprinted 1995

© Elspeth King 1985

All rights reserved. No part of this publication may be
reproduced, stored in a retrieval system, or transmitted,
in any form or by any means, electronic, mechanical,
photocopying, recording or otherwise, without the prior
permission of W & R Chambers Ltd.

British Library Cataloguing in Publication Data

A catalogue record for this book is
available from the British Library

ISBN 0-550-22560-9

Front cover: Photograph courtesy of Eric Thorburn
Back cover: Section from the Glasgow History Mural by Ken Currie

Printed and bound in Great Britain by Cox & Wyman Ltd, Reading

Contents

Map of the Glasgow Green area   6

Acknowledgements   8

 1. The People's Palace   9

 2. Glasgow Green   19

 3. Glasgow Green, the property of the people   27

 4. Glasgow's Treasure House   44

 5. Industrial Enterprise   50

 6. Housing and Social Conditions   59

 7. Labour History   66

 8. Women's History   75

 9. Leisure Time   82

10. Public Art   96

11. Religious Life   105

12. The Glasgow People   109

13. Glasgow Green today   113

14. Sources   120

1. People's Palace
2. Martin Fountain
3. Monteith Row
4. Templeton's Factory
5. Charlotte Street
6. Greendyke Street
7. Castle Boins
8. St. Andrews-by-the-Green
9. St. Andrews Parish Church
10. City Orphan Home
11. The Tent Hall
12. Saltmarket

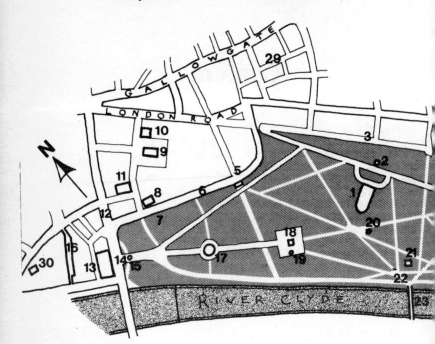

THE PEOPLE'S PALACE
and
GLASGOW GREEN

0   500m

13. High Court
14. Jail Square
15. Collins Fountain
16. Paddy's Market
17. Doulton Fountain
18. Nelson's Monument

19. James Watt Monument
20. Hugh Macdonald Fountain
21. Humane Society House
22. Arns Well (site)
23. Suspension Bridge
24. Fleshers' Haugh

25. Allan's Pen (site)
26. McPhun's Park/Daisy Green
27. Buchanan Institution
28. Logan & Johnston
29. The Barrows
30. Merchants' Steeple

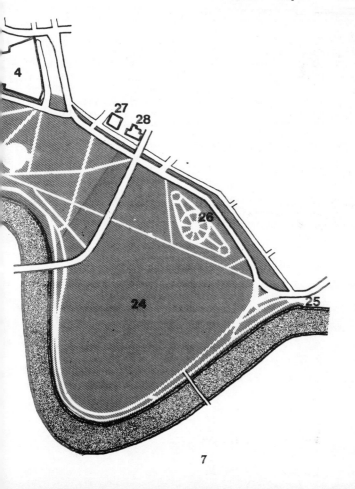

Acknowledgements

All of the photographs in this publication are from the collection of the People's Palace (Glasgow Museums and Art Galleries). I would like to thank Adam McNaughton, Alastair McDonald and Alec Jamieson for permission to quote extensively from or reproduce their songs. I am deeply indebted to my colleagues Michael Donnelly who read the text and made helpful suggestions and Irene Pyle who also typed it.

1

The People's Palace

The People's Palace is an institution which has been dear to the hearts of generations of Glaswegians and holds a special place in the affections of the Glasgow people. At the opening ceremony on 22nd January, 1898 Lord Rosebery expressed the hope that it would become "a palace of pleasure and imagination around which the people may place their affections and which may give them a home on which their memory may rest".[1] While it has done this and more, the philosophy behind it and the reasons for its foundation have been largely forgotten. Its story is different from that of most other municipal museums however and is worth recounting.

The People's Palace was over thirty years in the making. The intention of providing museum and gallery facilities in the east end dates to 1866 when over £2500 was realised from the sale of the old Bridgeton bleaching green and deposited with the Clydesdale Bank to gain interest for that purpose. Although the Glasgow Public Parks, Museums and Galleries Act of 1878 formally empowered the Lord Provost, Magistrates and Council to put the money to this use,[2] it took more than a decade for Glasgow Corporation to turn its attention to the task, and another decade before the site was selected and plans for the building got underway. Work started in April, 1895 and was almost complete by the end of 1897.

That the task should have taken so long is not to be wondered at. Glasgow Corporation was grappling with a many-headed hydra of slum housing, inadequate sanitation, rising crime, widespread drunkenness, ignorance, poverty, disease, epidemics and deprivation of a kind which was scarcely paralleled elsewhere. In 1866, when the initial deposit was made, the concern of the Corporation of Glasgow was with the Act setting up the City Improvement Trust to rid the city of its worst slums. Museum and gallery provision was scarcely a priority.

From the early 1850s, when the Town Council set about winning a fresh and healthy water supply for the city from Loch Katrine, Glasgow's civic leaders embarked upon an impressive programme of municipalisation to improve existing or provide new resources. Of necessity, much attention had to be given to public health and works — the provision of hospitals for infectious diseases; the inspection and control of meat and milk production; the setting up and management of refuse disposal and sewage plants. The provision of baths and washhouses, in a city which had so many single room dwelling houses without sanitation, was a high priority, as were the construction of sanitary washhouses, for cleansing and disinfecting bedding and clothing after infectious disease cases. The Public Health Department and the Sanitary Department, established in 1870, played a major part in improving social conditions in Glasgow, and it was from the latter that the Housing Department was established in 1919.

In 1869, when Glasgow Corporation undertook the responsibility of lighting the streets by gas, it also absorbed the private gas companies. Gas street lighting was first introduced into Glasgow in 1817, but with the supply in different hands, the service was unsatisfactory. In 1890, Glasgow Corporation also sought and obtained the same power with regard to the generation and supply of electricity. This venture was highly successful. In 1893 there were 108 consumers of electricity in Glasgow; by 1913 they had increased to 27,848.

Municipal control was a matter of common sense as well as political conviction. Glasgow Corporation continued to take on more powers and responsibilities in the interests of the many, and what was done, was done extraordinarily well. The star of the municipal programme was undoubtedly the tramway system. From 1872, the Glasgow trams were run by a private company and when the renewal of their lease came up for discussion in 1890, municipal control of the system became a test question in the local elections of 1890 and 1891. The voters were in favour, and the Corporation of Glasgow Tramway system was established in 1894.[3] Its success was legendary, and celebrated in contemporary music hall songs such as "Glasgow's Tuppeny Tram".

Glasgow Corporation also took on the telephone system, which in 1900 was small, inefficient, and costly for the subscriber. There were then 5000 telephones in the city, but by the time the Corporation was forced to sell its system to the Post Office in 1907, there were 40,000 telephones — more than were to be found in Manchester, Liverpool, Birmingham, Sheffield and Bristol added together.[4]

Glasgow's municipal control and its success was one of the wonders of the civilised world. Every year, visiting American professors came in numbers to "spend their vacations at the feet of St. Mungo" and to study and admire Glasgow's system.[5] In this respect Glasgow was not simply miles better, it was second to none. There was of course, much debate on how many responsibilities any local authority could reason-

Songsheet for "Glasgow's Tuppeny Tram".

ably undertake, and many speakers at the International Congress on Workers Dwelling Houses in Paris in 1900 for example, emphasised that municipal control of housing was impracticable. The Congress was shocked when Councillor Daniel Macauley Stevenson announced that far from being impracticable, it had actually been carried on in Glasgow, to an ever-increasing extent for twenty nine years, and moreover the Corporation also supplied water, gas, electricity and tramways. The delegates felt that this was "nothing short of rank socialism".

Daniel Macauley Stevenson (1851-1944) a prominent tea merchant who served on the City Council for twenty two years, the last three of them as Lord Provost, was no socialist. Like most of his fellow councillors he was a successful businessman and a Liberal with a social conscience. He looked forward to a municipal milk supply and the provision of a municipal health service, freeing the infirmaries from "the ignominy of begging from the benevolent the funds required for carrying on their work".[6] He and his colleagues believed in drastic devolution of power from Parliament to the local authorities, and Home Rule.

While these were aspirations which were also shared with the socialists who began to win representation on Glasgow Corporation in the 1890s, the difference between them was one of approach and political philosophy. The Socialists saw the "municipal socialism" of the Liberal Council in Glasgow as the foundation for a new society, and not as an end in itself.

The building of the People's Palace was part of Glasgow's programme of municipal provision. Ideas regarding palaces for the people were general at the time, but the original source for them was a popular utopian novel entitled "All sorts and conditions of men" written by Sir Walter Besant in 1882, and which ran to many editions. The wealthy character in Besant's novel sets about building a palace of delight and joy which provides "absolutely free for all the same enjoyments as are purchased by the rich" — painting, music, dancing, singing. The effect of this palace was to provide joy and happiness in place of "political wrangles". Thus one of the characters, Radical Dick was to be transformed from a "fierce republican" into an enthusiastic radical by dancing lessons. Singing lessons were then to change him into an "advanced liberal", after which lessons in painting would change him into a "mere conservative" with no political views at all.

If the members of Glasgow Corporation entertained such crude notions of social control, they did not voice them. The arguments for the Glasgow People's Palace were put forward by Councillor Robert Crawford in a paper to the Ruskin Society in 1891.[7] Crawford was both Chairman of the Health Committee, which dealt with hospitals, cleansing and sanitation, and of the Committee for Galleries and Museums. He saw one function as being an extension of the other: the Corporation of Glasgow was making provision for the physical well-being of Glaswegians, and ought to look after their cultural welfare too. Public health and municipal art were inextricably linked. Although some people thought that the working classes had shown no evident desire for art, he felt that cultural provisions were in themselves desirable — it had not been the dirtiest of the population who had petitioned for municipal baths, but when the baths were provided, the unwashed used them.

In building the Glasgow People's Palace, the Corporation took into account what had happened elsewhere. In May, 1887, the People's Palace for East London was opened in Mile End Road. The institution had its origins in the Beaumont Institution of 1840 and was largely financed by the Drapers Company and by money from a number of charities. It was managed by a private trust of influential individuals including Walter Besant. The nucleus of the complex was the Queen's Hall, a concert hall with seating for 2500 people. There were also refreshment rooms and a rotunda reading room, and a library, art gallery, music room, gymnasium, swimming baths, winter gardens and play rooms were planned over a number of years. The trustees of the project were acutely conscious that cultural and recreational facilities in London's East End were minimal in comparison to what was available in other parts of the city, and the chief purpose of the People's Palace was to "create and scatter pleasure" in an otherwise joyless area.[8]

In the same year, a People's Palace was opened at Bridgeport, Connecticut in the United States. It was built at a cost of $100,000 and designed to provide for the needs of working women.[9]

A large, grandiose People's Palace was opened at Zürich in March 1898 with a pavilion, concert halls, terraces and a restaurant. Overlooking the lake, it was built to cater for the needs of the large numbers of tourists and sightseers who thronged into Zürich even then.[10]

Other institutions have been called People's Palaces from time to time. While some Edinburgh citizens expressed an interest in establishing a People's Palace there in 1902, the institution which ultimately was graced with the name was a lodging house for the less fortunate in the Grassmarket. Similarly, in New Zealand, People's Palaces are cheap hotels.

The aims behind the People's Palace in Glasgow were similar to those of the London Institution, inasmuch as the common purpose was cultural provision for the working class people of the relatively deprived east ends of the two cities. In Glasgow however, where municipal provision was already generous, there was no need for the library, gymnasium, swimming baths and facilities for technical education that were among the main features of the People's Palace in Mile End Road. Technical education for the working classes had been an issue in Glasgow from the 1780s when Professor John Anderson began his lectures for artisans. In the 19th century, the Andersonian Institute founded by him, and the various Mechanics Institutes and the Decorative Trades Insti-

The winter gardens, "treasurehouse of the beautiful in shrub and flower", shortly after the opening of the People's Palace in 1898. The sculpture group on the left was Frampton's plaster for his work at the rear of Kelvingrove Art Gallery. The plaster disintegrated in the heat and humidity.

tute taught a wide range of technical trades. It is not surprising therefore that the London People's Palace developed into a polytechnic (now Queen Mary College, and part of the University of London), while the Glasgow People's Palace flourished as a museum, gallery, winter gardens and music hall.

The purpose of the Glasgow People's Palace was explained at the opening ceremony by Bailie Bilsland, an ardent campaigner for free libraries, free ferries, free art galleries, free museums, free recreation grounds and the extension of public parks. He had chaired the special committee which had supervised the work, and the institution was shaped by his thought:

> The general idea is that the permanent collections to be formed should relate to the history and industries of the city, and that some space should be set apart for special sectional exhibitions to

14

be held from time to time, in connection with which prizes may be awarded for works of special excellence. While primarily serving as a conservatory and a place of attraction during the shorter days, the Winter Garden portion has been designed and arranged to serve also as a hall where musical performances can be given to large audiences. One element of originality in the way of municipal enterprise that can be claimed for this institution lies in the combination, practically under one roof, of a museum, picture gallery, winter garden and music hall. So far as we are aware, no municipality in the kingdom has provided an institution combining all these features".[11]

It is because of this special combination of different features that the People's Palace has won a place in the hearts of the Glasgow people. There is no museum, gallery, arts or community centre quite like it anywhere else in the world. The Winter Gardens built to provide an area for popular musical entertainments as well as serving as "the treasure-house of the beautiful in shrub and flower" has given an enduring magical quality which makes the building unique.

The People's Palace was designed by Mr. A. B. Macdonald the City Engineer in the French Renaissance style. The museum portion which has a frontage of 100 feet and a depth of 40 feet was built with red sandstone from the Locharbriggs quarries in Dumfries-shire. It is decorated with allegorical figures representing shipbuilding, mathematical science, painting, sculpture, engineering and the textile industry by the Glasgow sculptor Kellock Brown. The Winter Gardens portion, measuring 180 by 120 feet and 60 feet in height was constructed by Boyd and Son of Paisley, and tradition has it that it was designed to imitate the inverted hull of Lord Nelson's flagship, the "Victory" on account of the building's proximity to the first monument in Britain commemorating Nelson. William Baird of the Temple Iron Works was partly responsible for its design.

Other buildings by A. B. Macdonald in Glasgow include the South Side Police Office, the Maryhill and Springburn Public Baths, the Sanitary Chambers Cochrane Street, Dalmuir Public Baths and Sewage Works and two bridges in Kelvingrove Park.[12]

He was unfamiliar with the particular needs of museum and gallery construction with some unfortunate results. A critic in *Building Industries* magazine complained bitterly about the cross light streaming from the windows in all directions and striking the glass cases, making the contents of some impossible to see. In the picture gallery on the top floor where there were roof lights in addition to the many windows, the glazed paintings could only be viewed with difficulty.[13] In order to cut down the light, six windows on the top floor were crudely bricked up and faced with sandstone at some time before the First World War.

15

Maintenance access to the balustrade was thus cut off, and this, combined with guttering blocked by pigeon debris led to two major outbreaks of dry rot which threatened the future of the building in the late 1970s and took five years to eliminate. Throughout this dangerous period — the metal and glass work of the gardens was in an equally poor state — the people of Glasgow made it known in no uncertain terms that the building should be repaired and retained.

The People's Palace Music Hall, as depicted on the front of one of its programmes in 1894.

From the very beginning, those who worked to open the building were astute enough to realise that existing galleries were largely patronised by the well-to-do. Bailie Bilsland described the Corporation Galleries in Sauchiehall Street and "the great pile of buildings in Kelvingrove Park" as "a sealed book to the mass of the population" and claimed that "the People's Palace has been thought out and constructed on more attractive lines".[14] It was no accident that George Walker Ord, the first curator appointed was a young man of 26 with socialist leanings and who had chaired one of Keir Hardie's first Labour Party meetings in Glasgow.

There was a great deal of excitement about and enthusiasm for the People's Palace even before it was built. In 1894 an enterprising impressario pre-empted Glasgow Corporation and opened the People's Palace music hall in nearby Gallowgate. The management made some grand claims:

"The People's Palace is the greatest success that ever has been-known in Glasgow in popular amusements. What is the reason? — a hundred reasons that are quite apparent to those who care to study the facts. . . . The prices are just one half of what is charged in the cheaper halls and only a fractional part of what is charged in the best. . . . No crowding allowed; no standing in the passages; no vexatious extra charges. Family night every Friday, when Sweethearts and Wives are admitted free. Special stair reserved for ladies and children. Lavatories on every floor, and a host of other advantages. English Opera has been produced here. . . . The Boxing Kangaroo and the Wrestling Lion made their first appearance in Scotland at this hall. Such enterprise does not go unrewarded. The independent respectable working class know who are their best friends. Charity is not in their line, but change for a shilling is — especially when value is given for a little more than a shilling — with a spice of civility thrown in. HENCE THE SUCCESS OF THE PEOPLE'S PALACE. We should have a dozen such Palaces. . . ."[15]

The shareholders of the People's Palace Company Limited were none other than Daniel Macauley Stevenson, Merchant, Samuel Chisholm, Wholesale Grocer (both of them Liberal councillors and Lord Provosts of Glasgow), William Martin, Shipping Agent, John G. Sharp, Property Agent, Malcolm Campbell, Fruit Merchant, Henry R. Taggert, Warehouseman, and James A. Allan of the Allan Shipping Line[16] (the "millionaire socialist" and ILP candidate for Dennistoun) — not the kind of people one would expect to have interests in running a music hall. The People's Palace music hall closed shortly before the People's Palace on Glasgow Green opened. Did these prominent businessmen take fright when they heard of this private enterprise, and buy their way into the company with the intention of closing it down? Or, more likely, did they take advantage of the popularity of the People's Palace music hall, nurture it, and kill it judiciously just as their municipal palace was about to open, hoping that loyalties to the music hall would be transferred to the new building?

In the early years, there were high expectations that the People's Palace on Glasgow Green would improve the quality of life in the east end of Glasgow. Before the opening, the "Evening News" published a humorous little piece imagining a midnight conversation between Nelson's Monument, the Gymnasium, The Adam Arch and "the new neighbour" on Glasgow Green. The People's Palace claimed to be "an epoch in the culture of the east", with an explanation as follows:

> If you walk down Gallowgate by night or day
> Or in crowded Calton Streets you take a stroll
> You are certain to discover on your way
> That the natives mostly fight and drink and loll
> There is squalor smoke and gloom on every hand
> And none seem to enjoy life in the least
> But I'll change it with the magic of my wand
> I'm an epoch in the culture of the east
> And the Corner Boy I'll nurture
> On the principles of culture
> Till he quotes from obscure poets by the yard
> And conceives a glowing passion
> For the high aesthetic fashion
> And against all vulgar failings is on guard
>
> If you scan the teeming tenements that tower
> Along the grey and grimy city streets
> You'll never catch the flicker of a Flower
> *They* never knew of Summer's choicest sweets
> Nor hear the lark a-lilting on the wing
> I come to set before them quite a feast
> And the city with my fame is bound to ring
> I'm an epoch in the culture of the east
>
> At the window of each room
> You will see a sunflower bloom
> When the learning of the people I've increased
> So just keep your eye on me
> And some wonders you will see —
> I'm an epoch in the culture of the east[17]

How and where the sunflowers bloomed will be seen in another chapter.

2
Glasgow Green

It is not an exaggeration to say that Glasgow Green is the most important historic site in Scotland. For 800 years, the Green has served Glasgow for a whole variety of different purposes, and the history of the Green is the history of Glasgow itself. The Green is one of the great battlefields of Scotland, for a thousand battles have been fought there – the struggle by different sectors of the working population for a living wage can be chronicled in the meetings and demonstrations held there; the fight for political freedom, first for "one man, one vote" then "one woman, one vote" took place there; different wars against social injustices, against the demon drink, and in favour of free speech (among countless other causes) have been conducted with the Green as their principal public arena.

Moreover, the Green has been Glasgow's playground as well as Glasgow's battlefield. The Glasgow Golf Club was established here in the 18th century. The Glasgow Fair was located on the Green for generations. Both Rangers (1873) and Celtic (1888) Football Clubs were founded here. The Green was the place where Glaswegians took their leisure, and it was during a Sunday afternoon stroll on the Green that the idea of the separate condenser came to James Watt. The application of this idea in the development of the steam engine changed the entire course of industrial and human history, and Watt, in a letter to a friend, later gave a graphic description of how it had come about:

> "I had gone to take a walk on a fine Sabbath afternoon, early in 1765. I had entered the Green by the gate at the foot of Charlotte Street, and had passed the old washing house. I was thinking upon the engine at the time, and had gone as far as the herd's house, when the idea came into my mind that, as steam was an elastic body, it would rush into a vacuum, and if a communication were made between the cylinder and an exhausted vessel, it would rush

into it and might be condensed without cooling the cylinder. . . . I had not walked further than the golf-house when the whole thing was arranged in my mind".[1]

It can therefore be said that the Green was also the birthplace of the Industrial Revolution. Watt's steps can still be retraced today; to mark the site and commemorate the event a large boulder was placed there in 1965, on the bicentenary of the occasion. There can be few other places in the world where the birth of such an important idea can be marked with such geographical precision.

Today, by walking around Glasgow Green from monument to monument, and visiting the buildings of historic significance on the edge, one can virtually re-tell the history of Glasgow. In spite of the intrinsic importance of the Green as an historic site however, it has been taken for granted and has never received the kind of Tourist Board promotion that other less worthy sites have been given. There are many historic places in Scotland where there is nothing — other than a modern visitor centre, built at great expense to sell souvenirs — for the visitor to see. This situation has been summed up succinctly by Glasgow poet and folksinger, Adam McNaughton, in a protest song about the Green:

> The tourists go to Bannockburn
> Or to Culloden Moor
> We wheech them through the city
> At seventy miles an hour
> These places just have *one* event
> That makes them worth being seen
> A thousand years of history
> Have marked the Glasgow Green![2]

It is not known when the Green first became the property of the people of Glasgow, but it was probably included in the grant which James II made to Bishop William Turnbull in April 1450. Most burghs in Scotland kept a common green or grazing ground for the burgh's livestock, and this was the original purpose of the Green. A Town Herd was employed until 1746 to look after the sheep and cattle. He received his wages from the burgh, and had the use of the "Herd's House" on the Green, which was probably no more than a shelter against inclement weather. The horn of the last Town Herd survives in the People's Palace collections.

The grazing of cattle on the Green continued until 1870. The grazing of sheep went on much longer, and in the 1890s, Glasgow Corporation was drawing in an average annual revenue of £42.10/- from sheep grazing, as well as benefiting from having the grass kept short in those days before the advent of the motorised lawnmower.[3]

Because of the grazing facilities, the early fleshing trade was situated on the Green. The large flat area at the east end of the Green, rented by the Incorporation of Fleshers for cattle grazing, is still known as "Fleshers' Haugh". At the west end of the Green, tripe and slaughter houses, tan pits and glue works proliferated. Piles of dung and the intestines of the slaughtered animals were heaped up to rot on the river banks. Fortunately, the Cattle Market between Gallowgate and Duke Street was built in 1818, the fleshing industries were moved elsewhere, and the Green was cleaned up.

The Green as we know it today was largely laid out in the period 1815-1826 by James Cleland, the Superintendent of Public Works and statistician of the city. In an effort to improve and upgrade the Green, he drew up a series of plans which were presented to the Council in 1814, and work commenced in the Spring of 1815. After the removal of the slaughter and tripe houses the first consideration was the raising of the Low Green (the part which stretches between Saltmarket, Clyde and Greendyke Streets to Nelson's Monument) which had always been subject to flooding. The High Green (lying to the north of the Low Green) and the Calton Green were swampy and irregular; these were drained and slope-levelled, and the public washing house which stood near Nelson's Monument was demolished. A new washing house was built in William Street (now Templeton Street) in 1821. The Molendinar and Camlachie burns were culverted.

Fleshers' Haugh, which became part of the Green after it was purchased for the city in 1792, was in a similar condition — swampy and soft, and separated from the rest of the Green by a deep marshy ditch. The Haugh was drained, and the ditch filled in, bringing it onto a level with the High Green.[4]

The Haugh was previously distinguished as the place where Prince Charles Edward Stuart reviewed his troops on the occasion of his unwelcome 10 days stay in Glasgow in 1746. The army of the Jacobite Rising arrived in Glasgow in a tattered state, and the magistrates were compelled to provide clothing — 12,000 shirts, 6000 coats, waistcoats, bonnets and pairs of stockings. The letters of demand are on display in the People's Palace. It was after the army had been re-clothed that the review was held — with drums beating, colours flying and bagpipes playing. During the review, Prince Charles stood under a thorn-tree, which, until it was removed about 180 years after, was known as "Prince Charlie's Tree".[5]

The extensive public works programme of draining, raising and levelling Glasgow Green was only made possible because of the great trade depressions of 1816, 1819, and 1826, when unemployment was widespread and those in the handloom weaving industry were virtually on the point of starvation. Relief Committees were formed and the unemployed were recruited to work on the Green in return for the bare necessities of life. Cleland boasted that none of those so employed paid any attention when "thousands of misguided persons attended lawless political meetings in the neighbourhood of the Green, where caps of liberty and radical ensigns were displayed".[6] This is not surprising; only 340 of the unemployed thousands were given work on the Green.

In 1820, part of the Calton Green was used to lay out Monteith Row (No. 3 on map) a prestigious housing development designed by architect David Hamilton and named after Provost Henry Monteith. Built on the northern edge of the Green overlooking the River Clyde, it was considered to be one of the most exclusive streets in Glasgow. It became known as "Doctors' Row" on account of its fashionable occupants. Planners' blight saw to its decay and demolition in the period 1950-1980, and in 1985, only one of the original houses remains. The site was rebuilt with small modern houses, 1981-1984.

Monteith Row was not the first or only prestigious housing development on the Green's edge. Charlotte Street (No. 5 on map) was laid out by Archibald Paterson, who was in partnership with David Dale. South Charlotte Street between London Street and the Green was reserved for self-contained houses with large gardens. At the north end, the street was cut off from traffic by elegant railings and a gate.[7]

David Dale, "father of the Scottish Cotton Industry" and builder of New Lanark had his mansion in the south west corner of this street facing the Green. In spite of a sustained conservation campaign, the house was demolished in 1954 to make way for an extension of Our Lady and St. Francis School.

The Calton district was Glasgow's first industrial suburb, and like other industrialists of his time, Dale saw the advantages of living close to business and industry. Many other textile merchants lived in fairly close proximity to the weavers whom they supplied with webs and paid on receipt of the finished cloth, and this made for a much wider social mix than has been present in housing developments since. North Charlotte Street was a tenement development for the labouring classes. This intermingling of the classes ceased with the great push westwards to new and better suburbs, set apart from business and industry, from the 1850s onwards. The removal of the University from High Street to Gilmorehill in 1870 set the seal on the fate of the East End as a purely working class district with the implications which this involved in building maintenance. Only one of the South Charlotte Street houses has survived, and is in a ruinous condition.

During 1826, trees were planted on Glasgow Green, walks formed, and a Ride and Drive carriageway of $2\frac{1}{2}$ miles was laid round the Green, at a cost of £1070. This cost was underwritten by subscriptions. Those subscribing £20 had the privilege of using a four wheeled carriage on

22

the Ride and Drive; £10 subscribers were allowed a one horse carriage or riding a horse for life.[8]

The first public monument to be erected on the Green was that in honour of Lord Nelson. It is 143 feet high, and cost £2075 to build, the money being raised by public subscription. The foundation stone was laid on Friday 1st August 1806, the anniversary of the Battle of Aboukir. The ceremony was a large one — 80,000 spectators attended, and all of the public bodies in the city were present, including the 23 Masonic Lodges. The ceremony began with a service in the Cathedral, and thereafter, a procession on the Green. In the foundation stone, a plate was placed with the following inscription:

> "By the favour of Almighty God, Sir John Stuart of Allenbank, Baronet, Provincial Grand Master Mason of the Upper Ward of Lanarkshire laid this foundation stone of the monument, erected by the inhabitants of Glasgow, in grateful remembrance of the eminent service of the Right Honorable Horatio, Lord Viscount Nelson, Duke of Bronte in Sicily, Vice Admiral of the White Squadron of His Majesty's Fleet.

> Who, after a series of transcendent and heroic actions, fell gloriously in the Battle off Cape Trafalgar on the 21st October, 1805.

> This stone was laid on 1st August in the Year of Our Lord 1805, and the 44th year of the reign of our most gracious sovereign, George III in the presence of John Hamilton, Esquire, Lord Provost of the City of Glasgow, and members of the Committee of Subscribers to the monument, which Undertaking by the supreme God prosper, D. Hamilton, architect, A Brocket, mason".

On account of its height the Monument was vulnerable. On Sunday 5th August 1810 there was a violent thunderstorm, and at about 4.15 pm the Monument was struck by lightning. The top 20 ft of masonry collapsed, and the remainder was in such danger that a military guard had to be placed around it to keep the public within a safe distance.[9] The damage to the monument was recorded in a painting (by Glasgow artist John Knox) which hangs in the People's Palace.

This particular storm showed the citizens of Glasgow the necessity of fixing lightning conductors to the buildings. Benjamin Franklin, on a visit to the city in the 1760s, had lectured on the use of lightning conductors, and it was with his encouragement that a conductor or "thunder rod" was attached to the tower of the Old College or University in High Street in 1772. The damage of the 1810 storm re-inforced his advice, and after the Monument was repaired, a rod was fitted.

After the improvements of the 1820s, the Green was a high-amenity area in a rapidly growing city where open public space was scarce. As the houses of the working class population in the east end had but pri-

"Scotch Washing". The illustration on the lid of the Glasgow Washing House snuff Box.

mitive sanitation, there was intensive use of the public wash house, sited on the Green 1732-1820, and in William Street from 1821 (rebuilt as the Greenhead Baths and Wash House, 1876-8). The area around the Camlachie Burn in the 18th century was known as the "Castle Boins" on account of the piles of washing tubs or boins in which scores of women tramped their linen. This method of "Scotch Washing", done with the feet, was always a source of amusement or moral concern to the English travellers, and is graphically depicted on the lid of the Glasgow Green Washing House snuff box (c1840) now in the People's Palace.

Old habits die hard. The Victorian clothes poles to the east of the People's Palace, erected so that the washing from the nearby public wash house could be dried in the open air, were last in use in 1977. Although the wash house had been cleared away fully twenty years previously for an extension to Templeton's Carpet Factory, women in the area continued to bring their washing to the Green to dry, following a centuries-old tradition.

The building of the magnificent Templeton's Carpet Factory (No. 4 on the map) in 1889 is a testimony to how the amenity of the Green was valued at that period. The City Fathers did not want the Green defaced by a common factory building, and James Templeton was instructed to erect a building which would enhance the area. He chose William Leiper as his architect, and Leiper chose to model his design on that of the Doge's Palace in Venice. Built in polychrome brick, Templeton's Carpet Factory is a building of outstanding quality, and apprentice bricklayers still visit the building as part of their training to study the various usages of brick employed there.

During their 90 years in the factory, James Templeton & Co. made carpets for some of the most important floors in the world, including government buildings in Australia and New Zealand and carpets for royal weddings and christenings. Carpet making ceased in 1979, and the factory is now a centre for small businesses.

Another fine building on the edge of the Green is the High Court (No. 13 on the map), built originally in 1810 as the Jail and Public Offices, to supercede the overcrowded Tolbooth at the Cross. The building was erected on the old Skinner's or Doocot Green, and with it came the public executions, formerly held at Glasgow Cross. Between 1814 and 1865, 71 people (67 men and 4 women) were hanged in public in Jail Square in front of the court. To "die facing the monument" (Nelson's Monument was the last thing on earth that the prisoner saw) was for long a euphemism for capital punishment in Glasgow. Of those executed on the Green, 12 were found guilty of robbery, 3 of forgery, 11 of housebreaking and theft, 1 of rape, 21 of murder, 1 of throwing vitriol, and 1 of high treason.[10]

In time, the prison accommodation proved inadequate. Duke Street Prison was extended, and Barlinnie Prison opened in 1882. In 1910, the Jail and Public Offices were demolished and the present High Court was built on the same site. Only the portico of the older building was kept.

The Tent Hall in Steel Street is another interesting building on the edge of the Green. As an institution, it began with the great evangelical meetings of Moody and Sankey in Glasgow in 1874-5, conducted from a large tent on Glasgow Green, positioned near Nelson's Monument.[11] The evangelical movement appealed to the working classes and the poor of the city, whom the established churches had failed to reach. In order to carry on their work in a more permanent form, the Glasgow United Evangelical Association built the Tent Hall, the largest Gospel Hall in Glasgow, in yellow sandstone on the edge of the Green. The organisation did a great deal of charitable work, and on every Sunday from 1875-1979 without a break, a Free Breakfast was served to the poor of the area. The building is now owned by the YMCA and the Tent Hall congregation meets elsewhere.

Only two buildings have been built on Glasgow Green proper — one is the People's Palace, and the other is Humane Society House (No. 21 on the map). The Glasgow Humane Society was founded in 1790 "for the purpose of giving encouragement to efforts for rescuing persons from drowning in the Clyde."[12] Unlike similar societies elsewhere, the Glasgow Humane Society felt it expedient, right from the beginning, to employ its own officer. A dwelling house was built for him on the Green, near the river bank, with a boat house beneath, so that no time would be lost in carrying out rescues. Part of the boat house was used for mortuary purposes because of the fatal accidents in the Clyde.[13]

Over the past two centuries, hundreds of people have been saved from drowning by the Humane Society Officers. For two generations, the work was in the hands of the Geddes family. George Geddes (1826-1888) was succeeeded by his son, also called George (1862-1932).[14]

In 1937, Humane Society House was demolished and replaced by the present building, and the work of the Humane Society continues.

3

Glasgow Green, The Property of the People

When James Paton, Superintendent of Museums in Glasgow, addressed the Museums Association shortly after the opening of the People's Palace, he pointed out that had the building been otherwise named, the people of the area would probably have prevented it from being erected. Over the century, there had been tremendous resistance to any encroachments on the Green, or any attempts to spoil the amenities of the Green. Paton described the Green as follows:

"It may be regarded as the central park of the city, and on every side it is surrounded with a dense population. The Green is esteemed as peculiarly the birthright and property of the people, and the east-ender watches over it with a jealous care which is almost savage in its manifestations. By use and wont, rights and privileges have been established on the Green — as sacred in the eyes of their possessors as they are shaky from the legal point of view — and the mere moving of an orator's chair from one side of a railing to another has been known to occasion almost a riot. The Green is the Areopagus of the east-end, although it cannot be said the frequenters of its sward spend their time in hearing what is entirely new. There the fervid Orangeman denounces unweariedly the Pope and all his doings, and nightly he goes over, point by point, against his Romanist antagonist, the whole argument of the well-thumbed "Hammersmith Discussion"; there the blatant atheist with ease bowls over the enthusiastic but simple-minded soldier of the Salvation Army; there the fiery radical pours withering scorn on the present Government; there the indignant but long-suffering rate-payer — who probably dwells in a municipal lodging-house and who pays no local rates, but who contributes liberally to Her Majesty's excise revenue — denounces the blood-sucking Town Council; there the pure minded teetotaler rails fiercely against the

A watercolour drawing of the Low Green in 1808. The wooden bridge which collapsed in the riot of 1821 is on the left. The wooden buildings on the right were cleared away in Cleland's improvements.

whisky shop; there every faddist, every crank, and every quack finds a stand and an audience. The Green area is a marvellous and valuable institution, giving free course and comparatively harmless outlet to sentiment and opinions which otherwise might sometimes attain explosive force. It is a safety valve which should find a place in every great community".[1]

Although Cleland, the city statistician and Superintendent of Works, demonstrated how portions of Glasgow Green had been sold or alienated, or other parts purchased to make it larger over the centuries, the evidence carried no weight when the local people thought they were being cheated out of their rights.

An interesting case of alienation occurred in the early years of the 19th century, and the site of it is still marked with a plaque today (No. 25 on map). Alexander Allan a textile merchant who had the mansion of Newhall on the edge of the Green decided that he would like unrestricted private access from his garden to the Clyde. Accordingly he constructed a "pen" or pend, under which those using the banks of Clyde had to walk to pass his house and garden. The Bridgeton and Calton weavers, furious at this high-handedness, refused to work for him and he went bankrupt. The following year, the Clyde swelled to a torrent and the "pen" was carried away in the flood. Strangely enough, it was Allan's relatives at a later date who saw fit to commemorate the event, and the plaque can be seen on the banks of the Clyde at the foot of Newhall Street.[2]

The most sustained and serious threat to the Green in the 19th century was the proposal, resurrected every now and then, to mine coal there. Cleland had had extensive borings done in 1821-1822 and he published his results in great detail in 1828 with plans of the layers. He estimated that there were one million, five hundred thousand tons of coal under Glasgow Green, which, if extracted at the rate of 15,000 tons per year, would last for 100 years.[3]

Glasgow Town Council, ever cautious, did not take up Cleland's suggestions regarding the coal. Why he should have pursued the matter so vigorously after having had the responsibility of upgrading the Green, is a mystery. Nevertheless, the need to realise the revenue came in 1858 when the Town Council found itself having to finance the purchase of the land for the West End and South Side Parks and the McLellan Gallery property. It was believed that the debt incurred could be wiped out by leasing the Green for mining. The plan was presented by John McDowall, who owned the Milton Iron Works in North Woodside Road and approved by a majority of the Council. While it was recognised that mining would result in subsidence — the ground would drop one foot for every two feet mined — "in a city such as Glasgow deposits to fill it up would be very readily obtained". In other words, Glasgow Green was to be turned into a public rubbish tip for a generation in order to pay for parks in the richer parts of the city.

The citizens of the east end were outraged by this rank injustice. Opposition to the plans was led by an east-end councillor, Bailie James Moir. His family had a history of radicalism, his brother Benjamin having been transported to Botany Bay for his part in the 1820 Rising. By the 1850s Moir was a prosperous tea merchant (known as "the Gallowgate Slasher" because of his low prices) with a seat on the Town Council, and it was he who gave voice to the public disgust felt at this move to rob the poor and pay the rich.

The feelings of the east-enders are summed up in a contemporary song, "Airn John", (John McDowall's nickname) which was published by Poet's Box, off Gallowgate:

> Airn John since that's your name,
> Let me say this to thee;
> Ye'd better try some ither scheme,
> An' let the green a be.
> Look at it yoursel John,
> Is't no dishonest wark
> O you, to sell the Glasgow green,
> To pay the west-end park?
>
> But honest men like you, John,
> Are unco laith to steal
> Frae big folk like ye're sell', John
> Ye're unco laith at weel;

Ye'd rather skin the puir, John
Who has nae second sark
Ye'd pu' the buttons aff oor coats,
To pay the west-end park.

If ye maun sink a pit, John.
Sink it in George's Square,
Or sink it in the Crescents John,
Amang the rich folk there,
An' they'll be highly pleased, John,
To see sic noble wark,
Gaun on amang thesel's, John,
To pay the west-end park.

If ye come to the Green, John,
Ye may expect a fecht
For a' the folk in this gate-en,
'Ill stan' oot for their richt.
Wi' sticks an' stanes, we'll come John,
An' fecht while we've a spark;
Ye'll never get the Glasgow green
To pay the west-end park.[4]

To drive the message home, Poet's Box printed another sheet stating the case both in prose and verse:

"Glasgow Green, with her beautiful walks, her refreshing springs, her traditional sights, her splendid views, her grandeur and majestic worth is she to be broken up, annihilated and swept from the face of the earth forever? No! It cannot be. Surely they will not deprive the citizens of Glasgow of the Green, which, for centuries, has proved so much benefit to them as a place of resort for pleasure; where youth can freely gambol, sport and play: where age can slowly bend their peaceful steps and breathe the fresh air of heaven. When our humble artizan, after a day's incarceration in the foul and poisonous air of the city, finishes his daily toil and bethinks himself for a stroll, where can he go but to the Green? If it were but for this alone the Green should stand unmolested, for were it not for the working man, there would be no West End Park. . . . Taking all the benefits of this noble place into consideration, we think it highly improbable that the authorities of Glasgow will touch it, save for its improvement and cultivation".[5]

The matter of mining coal was dropped, but raised again in 1869 and 1888.

In the 1840s, the encroachment of the semi-permanent circus and theatre buildings on the Green at the foot of Saltmarket had also been dealt with. The buildings appeared annually at the time of the Glasgow Fair and tended to linger, and some were brick and wooden structures. In September, 1845, a large petition was signed to get rid of the theatre buildings. Commercial jealousy rather than any serious threat to local liberty seems to have been the cause of the petition. The problem was solved when Anderson's City Theatre was burned to the ground in November, 1845.[6] Millar's building suffered the same fate in 1848.[7]

The intent of the Glasgow Monkland and Airdrie Railway Company to bring a railway viaduct through the Green in 1847 was much more serious.[8] Had they succeeded, the present generation would no doubt be dealing with the debris of this now unfavoured mode of transport and trying to restore dignity to the Green — if indeed the Green could have survived for a hundred years with trains thundering through it. A similar but more recent threat has been to bring the east flank of the Inner Ring Road through the Green, slicing past the People's Palace, to join with the Townhead Interchange, with a spur running southwards to Gorbals, going between Nelson's monument and the Doulton Fountain. This would have destroyed most of the western and northern parts of the Green, and whether or not the People's Palace could have survived such a construction is a moot point. From 1973-1981 a sustained campaign was fought against it. The GRIM NEWS (Glasgow Resistance to Incoming Motorways) was published regularly, and the Secretary of State deferred the plans in 1981.

As on previous occasions, ballads played a part in winning the fight. Folksinger Adam McNaughton who rediscovered the ballad of Airn John wrote a similar song with a pointed message for the would-be motorway builders.

> The East End weavers fought here, to get a decent livin'
> We fought to stop the railway, in 1847
> We fought to stop the coal mines fae ruinin' the scene
> We'll fight to stop a motorway across the Glasgow Green.
>
> There arenae many choices when cars approach a toon
> You've either got to keep them oot or else to slow them doon
> An inner city motorway's a concept quite obscene
> For Glasgow people want to walk aboot the Glasgow Green.
>
> You Glasgow District Cooncillors, its time to change your plan
> The Calton folk and Brigton folk don't want your Autobahn
> You can stuff your eight lane highway up — you know fine where I mean
> We will not have a motorway across the Glasgow Green![9]

On each of these occasions where encroachments have been fought, Glasgow Green has been cited as the inalienable property of the people.

In a smaller dispute in 1983, the local community council cited in their favour a decision of the Town Council of 21st June, 1576 that "na mair pairt or portioun of the commoun muris sal be in na tymes cuming set nor gevin in few to ony persoun or persones, bot to ly still in communitie to the weill of the haill tounschip" and that any feuing or alienation of common land, contrary to this statute in times to come would be "of nane awaill, strenthe nor effect, bot null in the self for ewir".[10] This has never been rescinded, although various parts of the Green have been sold since to suit the needs of the Town Council and the city. However, when people feel that their rights are being alienated, the weight of public opinion has been brought to bear against the parties involved. A spokesman in 1858 summed up the situation: "The Green belonged to our fathers, it now belongs to us, and in future it will belong to our children, and if we have the spirit of men within us, we will *never* allow such infringements upon our vested rights".[11] The Glasgow people still feel the same way about the Green today.

The function of the Green as a regular political meeting place in the manner described at the beginning of this chapter ceased with Second World War. While by Paton's time it was regarded as a safety valve, in the previous century it had had an explosive potential. It was here that the Calton weavers had demonstrated in 1787 against the cuts of 25 per cent on their rate of pay. These demonstrations involved the burning or destruction of webs supplied by the manufacturers, or of cloth woven by scab weavers against the instruction of the Union at the lower rate. One demonstration ended with the military opening fire and killing eight weavers.[12] Glasgow's first martyrs in the cause of trade unionism, they were buried in the old Calton burial ground in Abercromby Street, where the Trades Council later erected a memorial stone.

It was no accident that the new Military Barracks constructed in Gallowgate in 1795 at a cost of £15,000 to house 1000 soldiers were the largest of their kind at that time.[13] They had to be sited in the east end, in the industrial suburb, where political unrest could attain explosive force. The demonstrations from the time of the French Revolution until after the so-called Radical War of 1820, when groups throughout Scotland almost succeeded in pulling off a general strike, were of that nature. Government reprisals after the 1820 affair were savage and salutary. Eighty five people were charged with High Treason. Twenty three of them were found guilty, and three were executed — one (James Wilson of Strathaven), on Glasgow Green in front of the High Court.[14] The others were sentenced to transportation to Botany Bay. Thirty years later, Benjamin Moir, who was scratching a living out of the barren Australian soil amidst widespread unemployment, was writing poignant letters to his brother James, the Glasgow Town Councillor, telling of his homesickness, his inability to save enough for the passage home, and asking him to warn potential emigrants against the place.[15]

Nevertheless, such lessons were often ignored. A full scale riot took place on the Green on the occasion of the King's birthday holiday in 1821. During the day, a military review had been held there in the presence of the commander-in-chief for Scotland and an immense crowd of spectators. At 6pm, there were fireworks at the Cross and after dark, crowds of men and boys went to different rope works for tar barrels, which they rolled to the front of the High Court and set on fire. To keep the blaze going, they pulled up the wooden fencing from the Green and piled it high. This was done as a protest against George IV's treatment of Queen Caroline; working people everywhere were firmly on the side of the Queen. At 9pm, the magistrates came with a party of dragoons to stop it from going further. A riot broke out and the soldiers scattered. When the Fusiliers and the 41st Foot were brought out, they decided that a cavalry charge was the only way to deal with the situation. The rioters panicked, and ran for the wooden bridge over the Clyde which connected the Green with Hutchesontown. The bridge collapsed with the weight and pressure, and many fell into the Clyde. By 11pm the fire had been extinguished by the fire brigade and the riot was over. One man was dead and scores were injured.[16]

During the 1830s, the first of the organised peaceful demonstrations were held on Glasgow Green in favour of Burgh Reform and the extension of the franchise. These demonstrations, run by the Liberal Party and the various reform societies, were essentially pageants, held with the intention of demonstrating the respectability of the reform movement as well as its strength. Usually, programmes were printed in advance, with the order of the procession, its route and details regarding the various participating trades — what they would wear, the symbols, tools, products and banners they would carry etc. Two of these programmes have been preserved in the People's Palace collections, and others survive elsewhere.

Many of the participants in the great demonstrations preceding the 1832 Reform Bill, and again in 1867 and 1884 felt they were taking part in a great historical struggle. Badges and aprons worn, and banners and objects carried at these events were treasured by their owners and passed on to the next generation. Reform badges from the great 1884 demonstration were among the first objects acquired by the People's Palace. Memorabilia of this nature is still handed in to the museum; after being 100 years in private hands, a banner praising Gladstone and carried in 1884 on a pole which had served in 1832 was brought back to Glasgow Green again for preservation in the People's Palace.

The descriptions of the demonstrations show the ingenuity and inventiveness of the participants. The Glasgow Upholsterers in 1884 carried a full size bed, "the death bed of the House of Lords" while the potters carried model kilns on poles stuffed with smoking rags. The

Reform banner of 1832, showing the Press as "The Great Reformer".

THE NATION AND THE QUEEN ARE AT YOUR BACK
THE FEW MUST BOW TO THE MANY WILLIE;
AS THEY DID BEFORE IN DAYS OF YORE
IN 1832 WILLIE.
YOU'LL GET YOUR NAME CUT OUT IN STANE
IN HONOUR OF YOUR FAME WILLIE;
IT'LL MAKE THE TORIES A' THINK SHAME
OF 1884 WILLIE.
(THIS POLE CARRIED A BANNER IN 1832)

1884 Reform Bill demonstration banner, carried in the great demonstration on Glasgow Green. "Willie" is William Gladstone. The 1832 pole has not survived.

beautifully made model hand-warping mill, carried by the Glasgow Handwarpers Society, is preserved in the People's Palace. The Handwarpers had a rhyme on their banner:

> We warp the web and will not stand
> An intermedling lordly band
> Their web is warped, their lease is ta'en,
> The House of Lords shall not remain![17]

These great pageants usually assembled on Glasgow Green, then paraded on a long pre-determined route through the town, returning to Glasgow Green to break up into smaller parties where speeches would be made. The 1884 demonstration had dozens of different platforms at the termination of the march.

One of the delights of having a major demonstration on Glasgow Green was the variety of speakers who participated, giving the demonstrators a good choice of listening. When the terminus of the May Day March was moved from Glasgow Green to Queen's Park in the 1950s, the choice ceased, and since then there has been one platform and one speaker at a time.

It was not only during demonstrations that speeches were made on the Green. Every weekend, orators of one persuasion or another would go, often with a box or portable platform, and take up their stance at some point between Nelson's Monument and the High Court. None of these platforms have survived, but the stool on which the great evangelist John Wesley stood when he preached on Glasgow Green (1751) is preserved in the People's Palace collections.

There was a wonderful variety of speakers on the Green, and their talents were commemorated in local songs and poems. Listening to the orators was an education in itself, and members of the audience, incredulous of what was being said, would go to the local lending libraries, read up on the subject and come back the following week to refute the orator, often bringing the books with them as evidence, and citing chapter and verse. Many working class people considered Glasgow Green to be their place of education, and it was said that many Glasgow councillors and Members of Parliament in the first decades of this century had graduated from the "Glasgow Green University".[18]

Preachers and religious orators were numerous. The most famous of them in the late 19th century was Harry Alfred Long (1826-1905) who could always draw immense crowds. He was Director of the Glasgow Working Men's Evangelistic Association, and one of the chief Protestant representatives on the Glasgow School Board.

His fame was such that before he emigrated to Australia in 1886 (where he set up Orange Lodges and Rechabite Tents) his admireres presented him with a huge jewelled gold badge inscribed "GGFD" — Glasgow Green Faith Defender, "for defending the doctrines of grace on Glasgow Green for more than 20 years". They also had his bust sculpted in white marble by Shannan, at a cost of £115 showing the gold badge and inscribed with the number of votes (the highest ever cast for one man) which he gained in the Glasgow School Board Elections. The bust was presented to the People's Palace in 1901 where it has been on show ever since as a fitting public memorial to his power.[19]

Among the many causes argued on the Green, one which has long since been forgotten is that of temperance. Glasgow in the 18th and 19th centuries had a tremendous drink problem, the origins of which can be traced to the Malt Tax of 1725, which put up the price of beer, encouraging people to drink whisky and other spirits which were cheaper. The European temperance movement actually started in Glasgow when it was introduced from America by philanthropist John Dunlop (1789-1868) in 1829. The word was spread by the press of William Collins (1789-1853) whose printing firm flourished by printing Bibles and religious literature.[20] Now a large international publishing house, it still has its headquarters in Glasgow today. Collins' son, Sir William Collins (1817-1895), continued to work for the temperance cause, expanded the family firm, went into local politics and ultimately became Lord Provost of Glasgow. He is commemorated by a drinking fountain erected on the Green opposite the High Court (No. 15 on map).

The other fountains on Glasgow Green also have a temperance or health connection. The Macdonald fountain at the back of the People's Palace commemorates Hugh Macdonald (1817-1860) author of "Rambles Around Glasgow", a little publication which initiated the whole rambling and outdoor movement in the West of Scotland. It was moved to the Green from its original site on the Gleniffer Braes, where it had been vandalised. Sadly, it has been vandalised on the Green since.

Bust of Harry Alfred Long, the "Glasgow Green Faith Defender", in the People's Palace.

In front of the museum is the Martin fountain, erected in memory of Councillor James Martin in 1893. It was made in the great Saracen iron foundry of Walter Macfarlane and Company of Possilpark.

The most spectacular fountain in the city is the Doulton Fountain (No. 17 on map), made for the 1888 International Exhibition and moved from Kelvingrove Park to Glasgow Green in 1890.

It was designed by W. Silver Frith and executed by him, with the assistance of the students of the Technical Art School, Kennington, and

In the Glasgow Papers of this week there appears a MEMORIAL, from the DIRECTORS of the MAGDALENE INSTITUTION to the LORD PROVOST and MAGISTRATES, praying for the formal ABOLITION of GLASGOW FAIR. Attempts have repeatedly been made to call attention to the frightful amount of Misery and Immorality arising out of the Observance of our Annual Holiday; and it is hoped that the present well-considered movement for its Abolition may be entirely successful.

The undernoted Placard is here reproduced as a Memorial of a former attempt upon the Fair. In 1854, our "respeckit Ceetizen," SANDY M'ALPINE, published his counterblast against the Fair; and at the same time the "REFORMED DRAM-SHOP" was opened in Jail-Square. Mr. M'ALPINE's "Discourse" concludes thus—

"In the meantime, an' finally, my bruethern, I want ye—I want *you*, my Lord Provost—*you*, Baillies an' Cooncillors—*you*, Ministers an' Teachers—*you*, Elders, Deacons, an' Members o' Kirks—*you*, Faithers an' Mithers—*you*, Young Men an' Maidens—*you*, Maisters an' Workin' Men—I want ye to say whether this abomina-shun's to continue or no!

"Freens, Neebours, an' Fellow-Ceetizens, that's what I wuz gaun to say!"]

A Wonder! a Wonder! a Wonder for to see!
A Braw Coffee-Hoose whaur a Dram-Shop used to be!

FREENS AN' FELLOW-CEETIZENS

IN GENERAL:

An' you Foke aboot the Fut o' the Sautmarket in partik'lar!

WILL YE SPEAK A WORD WI' ME?

I'm an auld **WHISKY-SHOP**. I'm an Interestin' Relick o' anshient times and mainners. Maybe sum o' ye dinna ken what a Whisky-Shop is? I'll tell ye.

In anshient times—lang before puir Workin' Foke were sae wise or weel-daein' as they are noo-a-days, the GLAISKA FOKE, an' partik'larly the FOKE aboot the Fut o' the SAUTMARKET, were awfu' fond o' **WHISKY**. This WHISKY was a sort o' DEEVIL'S DRINK made oot o' GOD'S gude **BARLEY**.

It robbit men o' their judgement,	But they drank it.
It robbit them o' their nait'ral affeckshun,	But they drank it.
It robbit them o' independence an' self-respeck,	But they drank it.
It made them mean, unmanly, and disgustin' wretches,	But they drank it.
It cled them wi' rags,	But they drank it.
It made them leeve in low, filthy dens o' hooses,	But they drank it.
It sent them in scores to the Poleece-Office,	But they drank it.
It sent them to the Jail, the Hulks, an' the Gallows,	But they drank it.
Baillies an' Shiriffs, Judges and Justices, deplored its effects,	But they drank it themsel's!
Ministers preach'd aboot it,	But they drank it themsel's!
It blottit oot God's glorious image frae men's faces and hearts,	But they drank it.
It made them beggars,	But they drank it.
It made them paupers,	But they drank it.
It made them idiots,	But they drank it.

This Whisky, then, wuz selt in Shops, an' I wuz ane o' them. That'll let ye ken what a Whisky Shop wuz in anshient times.

TIMES ARE CHANGED NOO! Everybody's a Member of the SCOTTISH TEMPERANCE LEAGUE. Naebody Drinks onything but Coffee. So I've ta'en up the Coffee-Hoose line mysel'!

Come an' see me! Ye'll get rowsin' Cups o' Coffee! thumpin' Cups o' Tea! thund'rin' dunts o' Bread! whangs o' Cheese! lots o' Ham an' Eggs, Staiks, Chops, an' a' ither kind o' Substanshials!

FREENS AN' FELLOW-CEETIZENS! I'm no the Shop I ance wuz! I've a blythe heart an' a cheery face noo! Come an' see me!

The REFORMED DRAM-SHOP,
20 JAIL SQUARE.

OBSERVE! Nae Connection wi' the JAIL owre the way.

Temperance poster, 1854 for a coffee house in Jail Square at the foot of Saltmarket.

the Lambeth School of Art. Made in red terracotta, it was Doulton the china-manufacturer's gift to Glasgow for the International Exhibition. Its theme is the British Empire, and the structure is surmounted by a figure of Queen Victoria, presiding over the peoples of the Empire, who are represented as life-size male and female figures of Canada, Australia, South Africa and India. Unfortunately, it too has been the victim of vandalism in recent years.[21]

Conservation problems were first encountered in 1891 when the fountain was struck by lightning and the figure of Queen Victoria destroyed. The City Fathers contacted Doulton with a view to obtaining a replacement figure, but were informed that as the figures came "straight from the hands of the craftsman and not from any mould" a replacement would prove very costly. The Council decided that a standard urn would be an economic alternative, but the Doulton company was outraged at the idea that the very concept of the fountain should be thus destroyed, and paid for the replacement themselves.[22] Hopefully, similar sponsorship will ensure its survival on the Green.

A natural fountain which has long since disappeared was Arns Well (No. 22 on the map), sited on the banks of Clyde some yards to the west of Humane Society House. The well was formed in 1777 when the marshy ground in the area was drained and chanelled. The spring water was considered to be among the best available in Glasgow, particularly for making tea and adding to whisky. Arns Well was also a great beauty spot and meeting place. Many artists chose to paint the city from this particular viewpoint.[23]

The area from Arns Well and Nelson's Monument in the High Court was freely and commonly used for public meetings until Glasgow Corporation in 1916 passed a by-law prohibiting singing, preaching, lecturing and demonstrating in the public parks without written authority. This controversial By-Law 20 was not invoked until 1922 and the graduates of the Glasgow Green university were quick to rise against it. The man who led the fight for the freedom of speech on Glasgow Green was Guy Alfred Aldred (1886-1963), a prominent anti-parliamentary communist and anarchist and editor of the Glasgow newspaper "The Word". For nearly ten years, he fought to have the by-law repealed, setting up a Free Speech Council for that purpose. His portrait now hangs in the People's Palace. When the Tramp Preachers, a group which lived in poverty and tramped the country preaching Christianity, were jailed for 30 days in June 1931 for preaching on Glasgow Green, the matter was brought to the attention of the national press. John McGovern, ILP Member of Parliament for Shettleston, asked questions in the House of Commons, and when he pressed the matter, was forcibly ejected from the House in what were described as "disgraceful scenes". McGovern, Aldred and Harry McShane went on to hold public demonstrations in defence of free speech on the Green, and after the disturbances which ensued, were charged with assault, mobbing and rioting.[24]

Although the offensive by-law was amended in June 1932, allowing meetings and literature sales in certain parts of the Green without prior permission, political customs were changing. Outdoor meetings were becoming less popular, and political debates could be heard on the wireless. Today, the demonstrations which take place on the Green usually have permission in advance from Glasgow District Council.

The Trongate of Glasgow by John Knox, 1826.

Chapter

4

Glasgow's Treasure House

From the very beginning, important paintings and items relating to Glasgow's history were shown in the People's Palace. John Knox's famous painting of the Trongate, 1826, has hung in the People's Palace almost without a break since 1898. The series of watercolours of Glasgow in the 1840s, painted by William "Crimea" Simpson (1823-1899) in the last years of his life from his early sketch books have been exhibited regularly in the People's Palace from their completion in 1899.

Nevertheless, the main local history collections were kept and exhibited in what was known as the "Glasgow Room" of the Art Gallery at Kelvingrove, until the gift of the Scott collection of European arms and armour in 1940 dictated that additional space had to be found. The local history collection was then moved to the People's Palace,[1] to join the other Glasgow memorabilia kept there, including the collection of the Old Glasgow Club. Since 1940, the People's Palace has been the official repository of all things relating to old Glasgow, and the treasure house of things past.

The approach to collecting Glasgow's past was for generations lacking in any systematic method, and the response to the demolition and changes in the old city centre, brought about by the City Improvement Act of 1866, was a typically antiquarian one. Carved and inscribed stones from the pre-Reformation prebendal manses and from the 16th and 17th century tenements were collected in considerable numbers, even although some of them were badly worn and barely legible. Whenever one of the regality stones which marked the boundary of the old city was threatened by development, it was acquired for the museum collections. The carved keystone heads from the Tontine building at Glasgow Cross, demolished in 1911, were traced and collected. The very large stone marking the place from which Mary Queen of Scots viewed the Battle of Langside in 1568 was also taken into the care of the museum.

Stones from buildings, when collected without photographs and ancillary data, and even basic information on the location of the site, are difficult to display and interpret. The opportunity of collecting from the interiors of buildings was rarely taken, although some splendid carvings from the interior of the Adam-designed Athenaeum building in George Square were rescued by a local demolisher and later presented to the museum. In recent years however, interior fittings have been rescued from doomed historic buildings such as the 17th century mansion house of the Dean of Guild in Stockwell Street (1976), the 18th century Dreghorn Mansion in Clyde Street (1978) and the 1902 Palace Theatre in Main Street Gorbals (1979) for full-scale displays in the museum.

Nevertheless, the antiquarian approach in the early days was paramount. Often when a building was being demolished, enterprising woodworkers would set up a small side-line in souvenirs. Snuffboxes, walking sticks and trinkets were manufactured, and these were later welcomed into the museum collections. The People's Palace has many items made of the wood of the Cathedral roof (renewed 1910-1912)[2] and of the mediaeval Stockwell bridge (demolished 1850). A local antiquarian who found a key jammed in one of the buttresses of the bridge had it lovingly displayed in a case carved from the famous Wallace oak tree at Elderslie (felled in 1856) and lined with red velvet from the clothing of a soldier who was killed at the battle of Culloden in 1746. It is now in the museum collections with the keys of a variety of buildings which no longer exist.

Prince Charles Edward Stuart's ten day visit to Glasgow on his march south to Preston is also commemorated in the museum collections by a series of demand letters for clothing and money sent to the Glasgow magistrates. After the army was re-clothed at Glasgow's expense, Prince Charles reviewed his troops on the Green. The coat of 18th century tartan in the museum collections which purports to be Prince Charlie's is probably quite spurious however; it was made to fit a very small person, possibly a child.

Many other relics relating to the history of the Green have become part of the museum collections. A Roman Samian ware bowl, dating from 150 A.D. and found on Fleshers' Haugh in 1876 is the earliest artefact associated with the Green. The stool on which John Wesley stood to preach his sermon on Glasgow Green is also on permanent display, as is the large burrwood snuffbox of the Glasgow Green Washing House Keeper, which has a scene on the lid depicting "Scotch Washing".

A sad reminder of the great disaster which happened when the walls of Templeton's Carpet Factory, then under construction, collapsed, 1st November, 1889, killing 29 women and girls in the temporary weaving sheds beneath it, is the little Templeton Disaster Bible, one of hundreds

The "dead" or "skellet" bell, rung for funerals in Glasgow.

issued to grieving relatives. An ordinary Bible, issued to a pupil of the Buchanan Institution, 47 Greenhead Street (No. 27 on map) commemorates this nearby charitable institute which was established in the 1850s to aid destitute boys.

Some of the early antiquities, while of a miscellaneous nature, are fascinating. Glasgow's "dead" or "skellet" bell of 1641, used during burial processions in the town and made to replace the ancient bell of St. Mungo, survives in the People's Palace. It is cast with the Glasgow Coat of Arms which includes a depiction of the Celtic-shaped bell which it replaced.

The huge Katherine bell which is almost 8 feet in circumference, and was cast in the Netherlands in 1553, is the only pre-Reformation bell to survive in Glasgow. It was last used in the Tolbooth Steeple at the Cross, but was probably made for the building which predated the 1626 Tolbooth.

The Tolbooth served as a prison, justiciary hall and town house from 1626 until the new jail and court rooms were built at the foot of the Salt-market in 1810-1814. Having 32 cells, it must have had a considerable number of locks, keys and padlocks, and every now and then "the padlock of the Old Tolbooth" causes interest in the Glasgow auction rooms.[3] Fortunately, the People's Palace has a number of such locks and keys, obtained by gift, as well as the barbaric "scolds' bridles", the metal harnesses used for punishing women in public outside the Tolbooth, or worse still, used in conjunction with the ducking stool at the Clyde.

Perhaps the best known of the Glasgow antiquities is the Saracen Head Punch Bowl, a large tin-glazed earthenware bowl capable of holding five gallons. The inside is painted with the Glasgow Coat of Arms and the legend "Success to the Town of Glasgow" while Bacchanalian figures dance around the outside. The Saracen's Head was one of the finest inns of its day. It was built by vintner Robert Tennent in Gallowgate in 1755 and was the first hotel in Glasgow to have corridors, giving separate access to the rooms, a great improvement on the practise of walking through other rooms to reach one's own chamber. For a generation, it was also the main coaching inn of the city. Distinguished visitors stayed there, as did the Lords of Justiciary on their Glasgow circuit, and the merchants and magistrates frequently dined and drank there.

The Saracen Head Bowl is a symbol of the days when excessive drinking was considered to be a virtue and an accomplishment. It has been broken and repaired on more than one occasion, probably during the great Bacchanalian revels of the first thirty years of its life. It was bought at the sale of the inn in 1791 by a gentleman who considered it to be a curiosity, and it was his grandson, Glasgow antiquarian John

Saracen Head Inn punch bowl, made in the Delftfield Pottery Works, c1760.

Buchanan, who left it to the museum in 1910. It was last used at a public dinner held by the Glasgow Archaeological Society in 1860, and an engraving of that date shows it to be in its present state of repair.

Contemporary interest in the Saracen Head Bowl is due to renewed interest in the history of Scottish pottery. The bowl was made in the factory of the Glasgow Delftfield Pottery Company, established on the Broomielaw in 1748 to supply both home and export markets. For many years, historians of ceramics refused to believe that such high quality work as the Saracen Head Bowl could have been executed in Glasgow. However, there is much evidence to the contrary. Among those involved in the initial promotion of the Saracen Head Inn were Provost George Murdoch and Alexander Oswald, and delft tiles from the house of the former, in Argyle Street, matching those found in the country house of the latter, at Auchincruive, survive in the museum collection. The quality of the work on the tiles matches that of the bowl, and it is inconceivable that hard-headed Glasgow businessmen should look to Lambeth or Liverpool for their pottery with a factory on their

The Roberton Hunt punch bowl, 1771.

doorstep. Sherd evidence, excavated near the site of Delftfield, confirms this.

The same evidence and logic has identified the smaller Roberton Hunt Bowl of 1771 as a product of the Delftfield factory. The Roberton Hunt or Glasgow Hounds, the members of which were mainly Glasgow merchants and local landowners was established in that year and in the minutes of 29th September the Treasurer was instructed to "bespeak four Delph bowls, to make a bottle of Rum each, with the Roberton Hunt written on them".[4]

Another important group of Glasgow artefacts is that associated with the various Incorporated Trades of the city. There are fourteen such Trades, and some date back to mediaeval times, while others came to prominence in the 16th and 17th centuries. They are the Hammermen, Fleshers, Weavers, Coopers, Barbers, Tailors, Bonnetmakers and Dyers, Masons, Skinners, Bakers, Maltmen, Cordiners, Wrights and Maltsters.

Several of the Trades have deposited their charter chests and boxes into the care of the People's Palace. Most of these boxes have two or three locks, the keys for which were kept by different office-bearers to avoid any irregularities in administration. The boxes date from the 17th and 18th centuries, and most of them are beautifully crafted.

Academic recognition of the importance of artefacts in interpreting the past in Glasgow came with the Scottish Exhibition of History Art and Industry of 1911. While the previous International Exhibitions of 1888 and 1901 had historical sections, the Scottish Exhibition, planned to raise money for the endowment of a Chair of Scottish History and Literature at Glasgow University, comprised the biggest loan exhibition of historical objects ever staged in Scotland. The "Palace of History", a replica based on Falkland Palace, was built at Kelvingrove to house these objects and the thick two-volume catalogue is still used as a reference source by Scottish historians.

Some of the objects now in the People's Palace came from different Glasgow waxworks. There were a number of waxworks in the city at the turn of the century — Crouch's at 137 Argyle Street, Stewart's in Cowcaddens, Fell's at 101 Trongate and Macleod's at 151 Trongate. The catalogue for Macleod's Waxworks lists a collection of objects of which no modern museum would be ashamed, although collecting methods are now considerably different. When Patrick Feeney, alias "Old Malabar", the Glasgow character who had entertained people for a generation on the streets with his juggling, died destitute in a lodging house on 6th November, 1883, a waxworks proprietor paid for his funeral and laid claim to his personal possessions — his juggling sticks, Chinese rings, the cup which he strapped to his forehead to catch the balls which he juggled, and other items. These came to the People's Palace after the sale of the waxworks in the 1940s.[5]

5
Industrial Enterprise

The People's Palace is not a museum of industrial history, having little space to collect and display machinery. Nevertheless, within the confines of social history it is possible to obtain an idea of the kind of industrial enterprise which made Glasgow the Second City of the British Empire.

Glasgow's industrial development was founded upon the tobacco trade of the 18th century when the advantage of the shorter shipping time between the city and the American Colonies (20 days less than the voyage from London to Virginia) was exploited to the full. Glasgow became one of the main entrepots for tobacco; it is estimated that before the American Wars of Independence, half the tobacco imported into Europe was coming through Glasgow for redistribution.

Many personal fortunes were made by Glasgow's "Tobacco Lords" and there were artistic and cultural benefits for the town in their support for the Foulis Academy of the Fine Arts, (which pre-dated the Royal Academy of London) and for the various printing and newspaper establishments. A splendid portrait of one of the most famous of the tobbaco lords, John Glassford of Douglaston (1715-1783) and his family, painted by McLauchlin of the Foulis Academy, is on permanent display in the People's Palace. Calculated to show Glassford's wealth, the portrait was painted in one of the main rooms of the Shawfield mansion, his town house in Trongate. A mirror in the painting reflects the scene in Trongate while a window shows an extensive park stocked with deer at the back of the house. Standing behind Glassford's chair and visible only after close inspection, is the figure of a negro servant which a later generation, no doubt with an eye on the anti-slavery movement, has attempted to conceal with the frame.

The trade in tobacco meant more for Glasgow than the accumulation of personal and private wealth however, the Glasgow tobacco merchants were not operating in a cash economy, and in exchange for

John Glassford and family at home in the Shawfield Mansion, c1767.

tobacco leaf, they were seeking to supply the colonists with the necessities of life.[1] The Delftfield Pottery manufactory mentioned earlier, was one of many outfits set up to meet the needs of the colonists, and every imaginable class of goods was manufactured in Glasgow to trade in exchange for tobacco. This diversification in manufacture was to prove a healthy base for later industrial development.

Few monuments to the 18th century tobacco trade survive, but three buildings in the Glasgow Green area might be mentioned in connection with it — the steeple of the Merchants House (1659, No. 30 on map), St. Andrews Parish Church (1739-1756, No. 9 on map) and St. Andrews-by-the-Green Episcopal Church (1750, No. 8 on map). The steeple is all that remains of the Merchants House (which was demolished to make way for the building of the Fish Market in 1873) and was used by the Glasgow merchants as a look out tower to watch for their goods coming up river by barge before the Clyde was deepened enough to allow vessels to come up to the Broomielaw. The two churches were built by the merchant community. St. Andrews Parish was modelled on St. Martin-in-the-Fields in London, and the pews and galleries were built from specially imported mahogany from the Honduras.² St. Andrews-by-the-Green Church was on a more modest scale, but it was the first Episcopal church to be built in Scotland.

Tobacco processing has been carried on in Glasgow from the 18th century to the present day. The older Glasgow firms of Stephen Mitchell and Company, J. & F. Bell and A. & F. Gale were absorbed by others in the amalgamations brought about by the Imperial Tobacco Company in the early years of this century, but the People's Palace has examples of their packaging. The museum also has a collection of many thousands of cigarette packets made by Mr. E. B. Basden between 1930 and 1983 and gifted by him. These range from the turn of the century to the present day, and new brands are always being added.

After the American Wars of Independence, tobacco was no longer the vital factor in Glasgow's economy. The demand for textiles and the ability of the town to produce them became paramount. Before the advent of steam power, the spinning factories relied on water power and were situated in places such as New Lanark, Catrine and even on the River Kelvin. A beautiful watercolour by Andrew Donaldson of the South Woodside Cotton Mill at Kelvinbridge (built 1784, demolished 1894) belies the misery suffered in this factory where the spinners had to rely on the power of the Kelvin, working around the clock when the river was in spate, or suffering unemployment when the river was low. At the Catrine Mills owned by James Finlay and Company, a double-faced grandfather clock recorded both ordinary time and the time lost when the water was not at full power. The mechanism for the second face was connected to that which drove the machinery, to ensure that no money was paid to the spinners when time was lost through loss of power.³

With the coming of steam power, some Glasgow firms specialised in the production of textile machinery for use both at home and abroad. The Anderston Foundry specialised in power looms, and the adaptation of Anderston looms with lappet-wheel fitments gave some of the east end weaving factories great commercial success. Before the lappet wheel, jacquard looms, which were complex to set up and costly to operate, had to be used to obtain patterned cloth. With the lappet wheel, however, patterns could be cheaply woven on the cloth, and this was particularly successful with muslins. The firm of John Lean and Son of Reid Street, Bridgeton, using lappet-woven muslin and astute business methods, virtually cornered the Middle Eastern market for Arab headdresses. The Arab headdress was the trade mark of their company,

South Woodside Cotton Mill on the Kelvin, by Andrew Donaldson, c1820.

MANUFACTURED BY

JOHN LEAN & SONS L⟨ᵀᴰ⟩

GLASGOW.

REGISTERED

Trade mark of John Lean & Sons with the Arab headdress for which the firm was famous.

which ceased production in 1962 when Japanese competition became too intense.[4]

The Glasgow firms which specialised in the dyeing of cotton cloth had even more success in the overseas markets. The Barrowfield Dye Works in the east end of Glasgow was set up in 1785 by David Dale, George Macintosh and others, with the technical expertise of a Frenchman, P. J. Papillon who introduced the process of turkey red dyeing to Britain. Turkey red is a process of discharge dyeing by which intricate colour-fast patterns usually in bright red, yellow, greens and blues, can be obtained on the cloth.[5] It was in tremendous vogue for bedclothes, curtains etc. in the 19th and early 20th centuries, and in India and the Far East it was used for clothing. Glasgow could not contain the demand for such cloth, and firms moved to the Vale of Leven, where water and suitable space for dyeworks was plentiful. The United Turkey Red Company survived there until the 1950s. All that remains intact of this once great industry is the collection of books of export labels, depicting Indian legends and meant to be attached to the bales of cloth. Usually, they are printed in Hindi, the Word "Glasgow" (from where most of the United Turkey Red Company firms ran their businesses) being the only indication of their origin.

Plate "Burung Kupu" ("Birds and Butterflies") by J. & M. P. Bell & Co. The pattern was registered in 1887 and was one of many produced for export to the Far East.

Glasgow is not generally regarded as a pottery town. No artist ever depicted a Glasgow landscape dominated by bottle kilns, yet during the 19th and early 20th centuries there were over 30 pottery works in existence at one time or another, concentrated in the Port Dundas, Townhead, Anderston and East End areas. Some of these, like J. & M. P. Bell and Company, the Britannia Pottery (both Port Dundas) and Henry Kennedy's Barrowfield Pottery, were mass-production outfits, employing hundreds of people.[6] Unfortunately, if it was ever made, no pictorial record of them has survived, and as most of the potteries had gone out of business by the 1930s, there were no public archives in existence to accommodate their business records. To complicate matters, many Glasgow potteries did not mark their wares, and some, like the enterprising Pollockshaws Pottery, Cogan Street (1855-1955) stamped their products "Made in Ireland" for commercial reasons.[7] Identifying Glasgow pieces, and trying to put together details of the city's ceramic history is not an easy business.

In the mid 1970s, redevelopment in Glasgow revealed several of the former waste tips used by the potteries. The most spectacular of these was uncovered in 1974-5, during the excavations for the new Buchanan Street Bus Station when mechanical diggers sliced into a former quarry, revealing twenty foot high banks of pottery sherds from several of the Townhead and Port Dundas potteries, and dating from the 1850s and 60s. All potteries produce a proportion of waste material which is perhaps badly printed or fired, or improperly glazed. These "wasters" were used not only to fill up quarries, but also as foundation material in the building trade and for road construction.

During excavation for extensions to an asbestos factory in Petershill Road in 1976 and 1978, a large amount of bottle wasters from the Port Dundas Pottery were uncovered. Some of these were transfer-printed for a beer merchant in Madrid. Similar bottles, made in the Barrowfield Pottery for merchants in Brazil and Chile, were uncovered during excavations for supply services in the Barrowfield housing scheme in 1976.

Glasgow-made transfer-printed earthenware and stoneware bottles have turned up in many places in the world — Western Australia, Zimbabwe, different parts of the United States of America, Canada, Cyprus and in the Middle East — as a testimony to Glasgow's enterprise in the face of fierce competition from the Staffordshire potteries.

One of the most interesting pottery tips was that uncovered during the excavations for Whitehill Secondary School in Dennistoun in 1974. The pottery ranged in date from about 1870 to 1900, and much of it consisted of hitherto unrecorded patterns from J. & M. P. Bell and Company's factory. The patterns were exotic, comprising strange birds, flowers and scenes, were often printed in two colours on the same plate, had foreign names, and were evidently intended purely for export.

About a dozen new patterns, in different colour combinations were recorded on this particular site.

In the early 1980s a Scots engineer working in Java and Sumatra began to notice Glasgow-made plates in the local markets there and assembled a collection of over 700 pieces, which were shipped back to Scotland. Many of these matched the sherds from the Whitehill site, and good examples were acquired for the People's Palace with a generous donation from Burma Oil plc. It was evident from the collector's experience that Bell's and other potteries in Glasgow had supplied a significant proportion of the pottery requirements of those Far Eastern islands — a testimony to Glasgow's business acumen and enterprise in those days of sailing ships and primitive communications. Shipping pottery half way round the world to sell it on China's doorstep, (undoubtedly at a profit, for the trade continued for nearly half a century) was no mean achievement.

Nevertheless, when the activities of the various Glasgow iron foundries are taken into consideration, the export pottery pales into insignificance. Glasgow firms exported metal fittings, pipes and constructional and architectural ironwork ranging from small fountains to entire palaces. The most prominent firm in the field of architectural castings was that of Walter Macfarlane and Company who started in business in Saracen Lane off Gallowgate in 1850. Expanding business necessitated a move to Anderston in 1862, and in 1869, the firm acquired several acres in Possil.[8] The Saracen Foundry earned a well deserved reputation for the quality and utility of their castings, and besides supplying bridges, lamp posts, street furniture and ornamental bandstands and other park and seaside furniture for towns and cities all over Britain, they built up a world-wide market for their products. Cast iron constructions were particularly suited to warm climates, and the sectional castings were made with a precision which enabled easy assembly when they reached their destination.

Perhaps the most famous of the Saracen Foundry's commissions was that for the Durbar Palace in Quatar, India, completed by 1912. The stained glass for the Palace was also supplied by a Glasgow firm, that of Oscar Paterson. Other overseas showpieces by Saracen included a railway station for São Paulo, Brazil.[9]

Saracen's ornamental ironwork has stood the test of time and the little diamond trade mark "Walter Macfarlane & Co. Saracen Foundry, Glasgow" can still be found on ironwork all over the world. Occasionally, news is heard of accidents to fountains and bandstands abroad, when communities write to Walter Macfarlane, Glasgow in the hope of having repairs undertaken.

Ornamental cast iron was a casualty of the Second World War, when railings and gates were torn out everywhere to feed the cupolas in the massive but misplaced salvage drive. Foundry workers recognised that

The gates of Walter Macfarlane & Co's Saracen Foundry at Possil, c1900.

Interior of the Durbar Palace, Quatar, by Walter Macfarlane & Co.

the raw material obtained from such destruction was negligible and that the benefits as regards the war effort were largely psychological. At the same time, ornamental ironwork went out of fashion. In 1939, Alex Hammond, a Saracen draughtsman was working on designs for new gates for a royal palace in Mysore. Surmounted by elephants, the design was largely Victorian in style, although the gates were to be operated electronically. Another design on his drawing board was for a bedroom in a house in Pollokshields, where the bed, raised on a dais, was surrounded by a cast iron deco railing and gates. Such frivolity was not in the spirit of post-war austerity; the Saracen Foundry was demolished in 1967. The two drawings are in the People's Palace collections.

It was the quality of the castings produced in Glasgow which attracted companies such as Singer's sewing machines to the city. Singers came to Glasgow in the late 1850s and opened a large manufactory in Bridgeton in 1871; in the space of ten years, the company had outgrown the site and moved to Clydebank.

One of Singer's agents branched out on his own and set up a factory for the production of sewing machines in Anderston in 1867. This firm, Kimball and Morton, were well known for their manufacture of "Lion" sewing machines, where the main body of the machine was in the shape of a lion, concealing the working parts. The People's Palace has two of these fine machines — a treadle of 1867, where the lion has a hinged "cage" to protect it when not in use, and a 1903 hand operated machine, where the lion's paws swing out to reveal the needle. Kimball & Morton diversified their manufacture, producing wringers, cycles and specialised machinery for sails, belts, wagon covers, tarpaulins etc. The company folded in 1955.[10]

6
Housing and Social Conditions

Glasgow achievements in the fields of industry, engineering, ship and locomotive building, and in exports, were won at a price. The people who laboured in these fields, and the people who flocked to the city in search of work in the 19th and early 20th centuries were housed in the most wretched and insanitary of conditions, with no health care or social services, and almost always compelled to work long hours in dreadful conditions for little money.

Defoe in 1727 had described Glasgow as "one of the cleanliest, most beautiful and best built cities of Great Britain". The buildings thus described had become slums by the mid 19th century, simply because they were not designed to accommodate an industrial population. The merchants who had lived in Stockwell Street and Bridgegate in the 16th and 17th centuries moved elsewhere, and their commodious properties were divided and sub-divided, with whole families living in single rooms without water or sanitation.

Among the worst places in Glasgow were the low or common lodging houses which accommodated the shifting population of the city, and those who had fallen on hard times. "Hawkie", alias William Cameron, left a description of some of them in his autobiography. In the "Flea Barracks" in Old Wynd, most lodgers slept on the floor. In a lodging house in the New Vennel, Hawkie had to share a bed with three others, including a married couple. In Billy Toye's lodging house, also in the Old Wynd, the place was overrun by rats, and Hawkie slept for nine months on the meat chest in the kitchen to protect its contents. On one occasion in the same house, he had to share the garret with a corpse, which was attacked by rats, and Hawkie sought the help of the lodging house keeper:

> "When we examined the body, we found, that besides the eyes, the throat was eaten, and the body all mangled. Billy could not get a

"Hawkie" the beggar and balladeer who left a rich description of street life and low lodging houses in Glasgow in the first half of the 19th century.

coffin from 'the Session' as he was known to be in good circumstances. That day and night we watched the body, and we had enough to do to keep the rats off it with a stick.... At last the corpse was carried on a hurley to the Police Office, and what became of it I never knew".[1]

Often industrial buildings were taken over and hastily converted into apartments to accommodate the poor who could afford nothing better. Sometimes, these buildings fell into such a state of disrepair that hasty demolition was necessary. This happened in the case of the Factory Land, a former carpet factory in Havannah, the three floors of which had been converted into 39 dwelling houses holding as many as 400 people in total. A visitation of it prior to demolition was described in great detail in the *Glasgow Herald*, 23rd January, 1852:

"Here was a den of filth and abomination, the miasma from which would have turned anyone but those bent on the examination of the premises as a duty. . . . The lobbies which in some cases are so narrow that two men cannot pass at once, were covered in every part with filth of every description and so thick and hardened that it appeared as if it would require a man with a pick axe to remove it. . . . In the 39 dwellings there were not more than 6 beds and with two exceptions, these were of such a character that we would consider them unfit for the use of the most vile and abandoned. In the others, all the apology for a bed was a bundle of shavings or straw, and although there were found from 2-3 inmates in the rooms, we were credibly informed that these hovels gave a shelter to no fewer than 10 and sometimes 12 and 14 human beings — stretched of course indiscriminately on the floor and preventing, while in that position, all egress or ingress.

In this great barracks there was not the vestige of water, for the fact that the inmates are so fond of whisky, they will not pay for this simple element. Jaw boxes there were none, but we are informed these domestic conveniences were at one time supplied to the tenement, but as they had become receptacles for every manner of filth, they had to be removed . . . now instead of throwing filth into the jawboxes, the inmates pitch it over their windows into the back court, causing, as it may be supposed, a perfect dungstead, the odours of which find their way into the apartments of all the occupants."

Such slums were the breeding grounds of disease and epidemics including smallpox, typhus and worst of all, cholera. Glasgow suffered severe epidemics of cholera in 1832, 1848-9 and 1853-4 while typhus was described as being an "active volcano" with periods of deceptive repose alternating with violent erruption. The Glasgow Improvements Act of 1866 saw the establishment of the City Improvement Trust and the initiation of the first extensive programme of slum clearance and re-housing. The Trust also turned its attention to the problem of the low lodging houses, and by 1884 had built seven "model" lodging houses. The facilities provided by these lodging houses — personal cubicles, with a bed and space for clothing, the use of a locker, the use of cooking utensils in the communal kitchen, the use of lavatories, baths, laundry facilities, a provisions shop and a recreation room — were unknown in the low lodging house.[2]

Some of the original model lodging houses, administered by Glasgow Corporation, saw service for over a century. The Abercromby Street model, built in 1878, continued in use until 1980. Before demolition, a typical cubicle and its furniture was removed to the People's Palace and while museum visitors may suppress a shuddder at the thought of

Tickets from ticketed houses. Above — the tin tickets of 1866.
Below — the cast iron tickets of 1900.

people living in such conditions, the Corporation model lodging houses were veritable palaces compared to those they supplanted. The cubicle in the museum remains as a monument to the municipal philanthropy prevalent in Glasgow in these times.

The housing problems in Glasgow at the time of the 1866 Act were vast, and desperate measures were taken to deal with them. In an attempt to reduce overcrowding and control typhus, the smaller dwelling houses were identified, measured and ticketed, a ticket or tin plate being affixed to the door stating the cubic footage and the number of adults permitted to live in the house. In 1870, the alloted space per adult was 300 cubic feet; in 1890 it was raised to 400 cubic feet. A child under the age of eight was counted as half an adult. The first tickets were made of tin and the numbers were painted on, but later tickets were of cast iron to ensure that the numbers would not be changed illegally.[3]

By 1914, 22,000 houses were ticketed and supervised by Glasgow Corporation Sanitary Department. Six special inspectors were employed for the purpose of inspecting these houses between the hours of 11.30pm and 5am, checking for overcrowding. Where houses were slightly overcrowded, the occupants were warned, but where there was a 30% infringement, the tenant of the house was prosecuted.

Glasgow for generations was notorious for these ticketed, single room or "single end" dwelling houses and the struggle to control or eliminate them was a protracted one.[4] Nevertheless, where the single room dwellings were built as part of the four storey sandstone tenements which were constructed in Glasgow from the 1840s until 1914 (as opposed to being constructed inside a factory or industrial building) the design was generally a good one. With the exception of the sanitation, the provision in the single ends in the traditional tenements was as good as anything offered by modern housebuilders, and in some cases, superior.

The sink was usually situated beside the window. Made of black cast metal and supplied with a brass swan-necked kran or tap for cold water, it was known as the jaw-box. The Scots verb "jaw" means "to pour", but the name was also re-inforced by the fact that women also liked to lean out of the window, over the sink for a "jaw" or conversation with their

A Calton back court, photographed by Peter Fyfe. The woman with the white blouse is standing beside the sink which served the entire tenement.

"Old Bob" and the children at the playground in Bain Square, Calton, one of a number run by Glasgow Corporation Sanitary Department, c1914.

Hawkers and their barrows in Moncur Street, where "the Barras" continue to this day.

neighbours. Beneath the jawbox was cupboard space. The door of the dwelling was in the wall opposite, and usually behind the door was a recess for a bed, often three feet off the floor, with space for storage or a hurley bed beneath. which could be pulled out at night. Against one of the other walls was a sideboard and a coal box, with two shelves above (one the length of the room) for dishes and china. On the fourth wall was the range for heating and cooking, and a press with a door for storage. All of these items were built in, often to as high a standard of workmanship as can be found in modern fitted kitchens. Communal lavatories were provided on each storey of the tenement on the stairhead.

This type of provision, while adequate even by modern standards for one person, falls short of the mark when a family requires accommodation. Many Glaswegians had the experience of raising large families in a single end, and countless people even took in lodgers to make ends meet. The horrors of family living in such conditions are scarcely imaginable, when people had to give birth, be ill and to die without the kind of privacy which decency demands. Medical officers and sanitary inspectors condemned but were powerless to do anything about the common situation whereby a family had to eat and sleep in the same room as the corpse until the funeral.

Peter Fyfe (1854-1940), Glasgow's Chief Sanitary Inspector, made a superb photographic record of the Calton area where single-end dwelling houses were prevalent and where, because of their poverty, a significant percentage of the population was employed in hawking and in the rag and second-hand clothes trade, giving rise to the institutions which we now know as Paddy's Market and the Barrows (Nos. 16 and 29 on map). While most of his photographs are of tenement exteriors, they often show the inadequacy of the sanitation with jawboxes, evidently intended for the use of the entire tenement, situated on balconies and stairheads in the open air.

Fyfe's photographs, taken in the years before the Great War, show a lively community — the hawkers with their barrows in Moncur Street, the barefoot children in Bain Square and on Glasgow Green in one of the play schemes set up and supervised by Sanitary Department, the girls working in the chocolate factory in Well Street, women tending their washing on Glasgow Green.[5] The people in Fyfe's photographs are the people for whom the People's Palace was originally built, and it is fitting that his record is now part of the museum collections.

7
Labour History

With the working and living conditions of 18th and 19th century Glasgow being what they were, the development of a strong labour movement which aimed at either improving these conditions or overturning the system which produced them is not surprising. Glasgow is the birthplace of the labour movement in Scotland and the Green was its cradle. It was in Glasgow that the first effective trade unions were formed, that the first trade union newspapers were printed, that the Co-operative movement was first established and the Scottish Labour Party founded. The first Trades Council in Scotland was formed in Glasgow, and Glasgow was the birthplace of the European temperance movement. In labour matters, Glasgow has always led the way and continues to do so.

The use of Glasgow Green for labour demonstrations both official and unofficial has already been mentioned. This was not only a 19th century phenomenon: many of the key issues in the 20th century were aired at mass demonstrations on the Green — women's suffrage prior to 1914, the Rent Strike of 1916, the anti-Fascist movement of 1938, the UCS crisis of 1971, the Miners' Strike of 1984. It is fitting that these should be represented in the museum collections and indeed, the People's Palace has one of the most important collections relating to labour history in Britain.

Among the items of great rarity are some fragmentary minutes of the Calton Weavers Society in 1772, fifteen years before the massacre when the military opened fire on the strikers. The minutes show the weavers to be literate and articulate, and to have conducted their business in an orderly and democratic fashion. These papers were found in an old chest of drawers which had been sent for repair to a cabinet-maker, who preserved them out of respect for their antiquity. They are a rare survival considering the brutality with which the union or "illegal combination" was suppressed.

In recent years, myths have grown up about the traditions of non-

Emblem of the Glasgow Cotton Spinners, Scotland's most effective trade union in the early 19th century.

violence and democracy of British trade unionism. While the unions started from this position, when confronted with attacks on their livelihood and on their members' lives, they often had to resort to desperate measures. One of the most effective and most violent unions in Scotland in the early 19th century was the Glasgow Friendly Association of Cotton Spinners (1806-1838) which began as an ordinary Friendly Society but felt the necessity to operate a closed shop. Until the mid 20th century, one of the primary aims of trade unionism was to prevent wage cuts, which masters and factory owners tried to impose whenever there was a trade depression, often through using non-union labour. The reaction and organisation of the Glasgow Cotton Spinners union was described in a news report of 1821:

"Its object has been by all means to keep up the rate of wages: all male operatives have been made members of the combination, or means have been taken to remove those unwilling to be so from the mills by threats, by spoiling their work, or by way-laying them at quitting the mill; throwing vitriol on them, shooting into their houses, or maltreating them in some way or other; so that hitherto few indeed, if any have not become members. At entry they have been sworn to secrecy — to fulfil the mandates of a majority of the brethren in punishing workers at under prices, who are called "Knobs" — in destroying works considered incorrigible, and masters inimical to their designs — and in contributing to the support of such brethren as may have been thrown idle by refusing to work at reduced wages. They have received a pass-word "Ashdod" — a grip — signs to be used on the street, in the mill, etc., and in each work persons have collected in the name of charity, and sometimes by way of raffle, such funds as the secret committee of three ... may have fixed as necessary for the exigencies of the brethren, and for paying the persons hired for such desperate acts as the Directors have appointed, and which desperados are denominated "Colliers". These funds have been applied to the support of discharged or outstanding "Flints" or staunch brethren at the rate of ten shillings to single and twelve shillings to married men, per week, for a year. . . .

Such is the outline of a system to which, through fear, many have been slaves, and from which they long ago would have shrunk had not a set of men ... kept them in continual thraldom".[1]

Even allowing for exaggeration in the above report, this was an impressive organisation. The union kept the upper hand by sporadic outbursts of violence. In 1837, it was forced to call a strike against a reduction of wages organised by all the Glasgow cotton-factory owners. The strike collapsed when after four months, funds were exhausted, and the leaders were arrested. The charges against them were conspiracy and murder and while they were acquitted, they received seven year sentences of transportation on other charges.[2]

Transportation was sometimes a life sentence and more often a death sentence, considering the length of the journey, the cramped conditions, and the brutal treatment of the prisoners. The outcry against the severity of the sentences was such that after being detained three years in the hulks at Woolwich awaiting transportation, the leaders were released. Nevertheless, the power of the union was effectively broken. The sole material remains of it — a bannerette and a tray with the emblem of the union — are preserved in the People's Palace.

When the cotton spinners' union was broken, its paper the *Liberator*, one of the first newspapers to be financed and supported by a trade union in Britain, went under too. Only a handful of copies of this paper which in circulation rivalled the *Glasgow Herald* now survive. One is in the Scottish Record Office, another in the British Museum and two are in the People's Palace.

From the start of the *Glasgow Advertiser* in 1783 until the removal of the *Forward* offices to London in the 1950s Glasgow was never short of locally-published radical newspapers. John Mennons, proprietor of the *Glasgow Advertiser,* was cited to appear in court in February 1793 for carrying an advertisement for the Sons of Liberty and Friends of Man in Partick in support of Tom Paine, whose book "The Rights of Man" was virtually proscribed.[3] The advertisers absconded and Mennons escaped with a warning. These radical organisations, with their demands for electoral and burgh reform and their support of the French Revolution were considered to be a danger to the state and their members were continually harassed.

An interesting early burgh reform medal (1792) survives in the People's Palace. Made of silver, it is inscribed as follows:

Glasgow Society Friends of Reform

John Smith President

Be unanimous active and steady in asserting & establishing the Rights of Man, and be not weary of well doing, for by Wisdom, Prudence and Courage in due time ye shall reap, if ye faint not.

The word *constitutionally* has been inserted, as an afterthought between *asserting* and *establishing,* demonstrating the nervousness of such societies with regard to government reaction against them.

The second-hand wooden press on which Mennons printed the *Advertiser* from 1783 to 1802 survives in the People's Palace, for when Mennons sold the paper, its name was changed to the *Glasgow Herald.* George Outram later kept the press as a curiosity, but the radicalism of the newspaper had departed with Mennons. In the great Reform Bill demonstrations of 1831-2, it is said that the editor of the *Glasgow Herald* was burned in effigy on more than one occasion.

Political education of the working classes was partly dependent on cheap newspapers and literature and it was in the interests of the government to keep the newspapers exclusive, expensive and conservative through taxation. The fight to abolish the Stamp Tax (achieved 1855) and other duties on newspapers went on for over half a century. As the tax was on paper, some proprietors tried to avoid it by printing on cloth. The "Greenock News Clout" of 1849 in the People's Palace is a good example of this.

Radical interest in the freedom of the press in Glasgow led to the formation of the Glasgow Typographical Society in 1817, nearly 20 years before the Edinburgh Society and over 30 years before the Scottish Typographical Association.[4] The banner of the Glasgow Society is in the People's Palace.

The great political goal of the 19th century was the extension of the franchise, and often the activity and strengths of different unions are evident only in the newspaper reports of the franchise demonstrations or in the material remains of the organisation. The Glasgow Tobacco

Spinners, whose box still survives, were founded in 1819 predating the earliest English tobacco workers union by fifteen years. They were active in 1832 and 1866, and in 1884 they put on a respectable show in the demonstration with banners proclaiming "Tobacco and the Lords are Equal — they are both weeds!" A giant pipe proclaimed their intention as regards the House of Lords — "Smoke them out!"[5]

Many banners in the People's Palace collections can be traced to the franchise demonstrations. Four date from 1832, and those of the Glasgow Upholsterers Society, the Glasgow Shipwrights Society and the Crownpoint Templeton Workers were made for the 1884 demonstration.

Surviving co-operative banners are of a much later date, although the first Glasgow Co-operative Society was in operation by 1830. It was formed by Alexander Campbell (1796-1870) a disciple of Robert Owen, and its first shop was in London Street. It was he who gave advice and instruction on the principles of dividends on purchases to the so-called "Rochdale Pioneers" who are credited with first developing co-operative principles. Campbell was ahead of his times in many other respects. During the Reform Bill agitation of the 1830s, he was advocating women's suffrage and organising a Glasgow United Committee of Trades, from which the idea for a Trades Council was later to come. He also contributed to its newsletter, the *Herald to the Trades Advocate* and then to the *Trades Advocate* or *Scottish Trade Union Gazette* which was suppressed in 1833.

Another of his newspapers, the *Tradesman,* he attempted to give away free to avoid paying Stamp Duty. In the 1850s after a period in England he came back to edit the *Glasgow Sentinel* and became chairman of the Co-operative Association. In 1858 he helped establish the Glasgow Trades Council, which still flourishes, and it was he who was largely instrumental in developing the Scottish Cooperative Wholesale Society (1868), which was to affect the lives of most of the working people of Scotland for a century.[6] Campbell is one of the great unsung heroes of labour philosophy in Victorian Britain. His portrait hangs in the People's Palace.

Glasgow was the headquarters of the Scottish Co-operative Wholesale Society (SCWS) until its absorption by the CWS in 1974. During its existence, the SCWS was not just the favoured retail store of the working classes, but also a vehicle for its political education and the watchdog of its welfare. It built up a vast manufacturing industry centred on Shieldhall, producing quality goods from cradles to coffins and all things in between, for its members at reasonable prices. People developed a fierce loyalty to their particular Society, and those who disdained the ordinary banking system could feel at home with their Co-op share book and quarterly dividend. Moreover, the Co-op was a good employer of labour and reaped the benefit in quality work. The SCWS shoe factory at Shieldhall made shoes which were reputedly second to none, and the pride of the shoemakers is reflected in the giant leather boots, made for the 1901 International Exhibition and the huge shoes (size 36 in scale) made for the 1938 Empire Exhibition, and now in the People's Palace.

The Co-operative movement spawned a whole host of ancilliary organisations — co-op choirs and drama groups, co-op guilds and a co-op party. Like other movements on the left with which it was inter-related, co-operation had the ability of providing for its members and followers an alternative society. Until the 1960s, co-operation and tem-perance were synonymous, yet the different temperance organisations had woven a similar network of social clubs, choirs, insurance schemes and burial clubs to serve their followers. Temperance was also big busi-ness however for manufacturers such as Joseph Dunn who produced aerated waters (the drinking fountain opposite the People's Palace (No. 2 on map), is still the symbol of the company) and R. Paterson who invented and produced Camp Coffee in Charlotte Street[7] (No. 5 on map). While the majority of socialists in Glasgow were teetotal, the reverse was not always the case.

A similar all-embracing socialist organisation which was very popu-lar in Glasgow was the Clarion movement. It took its name from the Newspaper *Clarion,* established 1891 and edited by Robert Blatchford (1851-1943) whose writings were instrumental in converting many people to socialism. The Clarion was a propaganda outfit which had the aim of making the clarion call of socialism heard throughout Britain. Clarion cyclists, clarion campers, clarion ramblers while enjoying the great outdoors and the companionship of one another had as their higher aim the spreading of the socialist message. While the organisa-tion has faded, the little community of summer huts at Carbeth to the north of Glasgow, established by the clarion campers after the Great War, is still in existence. The People's Palace has a collection of Clarion trophies, one of which was made at the behest of Martin Haddow M.P., who provided the metal for two unemployed Glasgow silversmiths to make it in 1904. The medals of champion cyclist Thomas Chambers (1899-1984) who started out in the Kinning Park Clarion Club are also preserved in the museum.

One of the main influences in political life in the West of Scotland in the late 19th century (taking into account the electoral dominance of the Liberal Party) was the Scottish Labour Party, established in 1888. Founded by Keir Hardie, R. B. Cunninghame Graham and others, it had among its aims universal suffrage, prohibition, Scottish home rule and land reform. It was absorbed by the Independent Labour Party in 1893. The Social Democratic Federation, which had a branch in Glasgow from 1884, was also an influential body.

The Independent Labour Party became a driving force as far as political education was concerned. ILP members set up the Reformers Bookstall in Glasgow in 1907 which became the main retail source of labour literature in Scotland before and after the Great War.[8] It carried a massive range of literature and published a 40 page catalogue for mail order purposes. The fine Glasgow-style trophy sponsored by the Reformers Bookstall for choral competition and made by Peter Wylie Davidson of the School of Art is in the People's Palace collections.

Choral singing seems to have been a feature of the socialist movement. The William Morris choir, and the various Clarion choirs are among those still remembered. The only choir to become world famous however, was the Glasgow Orpheus, founded by Sir Hugh Roberton (1874-1952) and made a legend by him.[9] He ran it with a dictatorial benevolence, and when he retired in 1951, the choir disbanded. Such was the loyalty he commanded that over thirty years later, the choir members and their admirers still meet on a regular basis, and have deposited their distinctive purple gowns, their newsletters and their memories, with a portrait of Sir Hugh, in the People's Palace.

Within the socialist movement at the turn of the century, there was a recognition for the need for education. Several youth movements flourished, including the ILP Guild of Youth. The Socialist Sunday Schools, which continued until recent times, were a prominent feature in the West of Scotland.

The great protagonist of adult education was teacher John MacLean (1879-1923), who began his political life in the SDF and who until his death conducted classes in economics all over Scotland. Maclean, the son of a Pollokshaws potter, was one of the theorists of socialism as well as being a great propagandist. He wanted to fight the war against capitalism, and not the capitalists' war of 1914-18. In 1918 Lenin appointed him as Scottish Consul to the Bolshevik government. Maclean's recognition of the potential for revolution in Scotland during the Great War and after made him a danger to the government. He was repeatedly jailed for his political opinions and so badly treated that he died prematurely at the age of 44.[10] As well as having a portrait and photographs of MacLean, the People's Palace has his desk and some of his personal items, including his university passes and literature from the Scottish Workers' Republican Party which was founded by him.

Another labour activist who is well represented in the People's Palace is Jimmy Maxton (1885-1946) the much loved Member of Parliament for Bridgeton whose powers of oratory were legendary.[11] The museum has a portrait of him by Patricia Fell Clarke, a bronze bust by Kathleen Scott, and a small collection of photographs and personalia such as a miner's lamp, auctioned in aid of the miners during the General Strike and later presented to Maxton. Other labour leaders who are represented by portraits or photographs include Keir Hardie, R. B. Cunninghame Graham, John Wheatley, Tom Johnston, Emrys Hughes and Willie Gallacher.

Desk of the Marxist revolutionary John Maclean.

Because of the political activity in the period 1900-1939, the West of Scotland was known as "Red Clydeside". While it is periodically fashionable for academics to deny the strength or the potential for revolution within the labour movement here, some things cannot be disputed. There were few other places in Europe which could match Glasgow's variety and number of labour organisations and the cumulative experi-

VOTE FOR MAXTON
AND SAVE THE CHILDREN.

'ublished by JOHN TAYLOR, Election Agent, 88 Canning St., Bridgeton
'rinted by JAMES HAMILTON, Ltd., 212 Buchanan Street, Glasgow.

Election postcard for Jimmy Maxton in 1922, the year that ten Red Clydesiders won parliamentary seats.

ence gained in fighting against industrial exploitation for nearly two centuries.

Another aspect of politics which is well represented in the People's Palace both as part of the labour movement and in its own right is the history of Scottish nationalism. The items range in date from Staffordshire figures of William Wallace (produced in the 1860s when the Wallace monument was planned for Glasgow Green) to a Coia portrait of the poet Hugh McDiarmid and include fascinating items such as the Home Rule stamp used by R. E. Muirhead to frank Bank of England ten shilling notes in the 1950s.

8
Women's History

An important aspect of the collections at the People's Palace is that relating to women's history. The collection began in 1949, when a group of ageing Glasgow suffragettes met to celebrate the 21st anniversary of the Representation of the People Act, 1928. Realising that as time passes, memories are shorter, they decided that the few pieces of memorabilia of the Scottish Suffrage movement which were still in existence should be collected and placed in the People's Palace. Although the collection is small, it is the only significant collection of women's suffrage material in Scotland, and one of a few in Britain.

The women's history collection is of particular importance in Glasgow where historiography and historical biography is largely male dominated, coloured by such sources as "Memoirs and Portraits of One Hundred Glasgow Men" (1886) and the Bailie's "Men You Know" series, which ran from 1872 to 1936. Glasgow history is often written as the story of the captains of industry, the architects, the inventors, the medical men, and the male trade union leaders and it is valuable to have objects and information which demonstrate the contribution of women. As regards the women's suffrage movement, the collection is of additional importance, taking into consideration the deluge of information published over the last two decades on the history of the movement in England which ignores the often central role of the Glasgow women in the struggle.

One of the earliest items in the collection is a rare medal of about 1840 commemorating the fight against slavery. The slave trade and the tobacco trade went hand in hand, and while Glasgow was never as heavily involved in the slave trade as Liverpool, it was not untainted; the 1830s and 40s saw the development of a very active Anti-Slavery Society in Glasgow which embraced many women. In the dispute which developed in 1840 when American female delegates were excluded on grounds of sex from the International Slavery Convention in London, the Glasgow society split on the "woman question". It became evident that the fight against slavery was the fight against male slavery only, and that white women were fighting for the emancipation of black men, who ultimately were to have more civil rights than all women. The medal depicts a black woman in chains supplicating a white woman with the plea "Am I not a woman and a sister?" It was from this point that women began to organise to petition for their own civil rights.

The struggle to obtain votes for women lasted nearly a century from the 1830s and from the 1860s onwards, massive petitions were sent to Parliament, and demonstrations and meetings were held. These had little impact before the advent of the militant Women's Social and Political Union established by the Pankhurst family. In Glasgow, the prominent members of the WSPU were on the left, and closely associated with the Independent Labour Party. The newspaper *Forward* edited by Tom Johnston, and the WSPU as an organisation started almost simultaneously in Glasgow in October 1906 and Johnston gave unflinching support to the women against entrenched male interests.

Many Glasgow women went to prison for their beliefs. The People's Palace is fortunate in having the silver prison badges of three of them — Maggie Moffat, Janet Barrowman and Dr. Elizabeth Dorothea Chalmers Smith. Maggie Moffat, a popular actress went to prison in 1907; her husband, the well-known playwright Graham Moffat organised the Glasgow Men's League for Women's Suffrage. Janet Barrowman went to prison with a group of six others in 1912, and the eightpence earned by her for two months hard labour has been lovingly preserved with the receipt and illuminated certificate signed by Mrs. Pankhurst. The Glasgow prisoners of 1912 published a little book of poems, "Holloway Jingles" on their release, and this, with the drawings for the front cover (secretly done on toilet paper) survive in the museum collections.

Perhaps one of the bravest of the Glasgow suffragettes was Dr. Chalmers Smith (1872-1944). She was one of the first women to graduate in medicine from Glasgow University, and took up a post at the Royal Samaritan Hospital for Women on the south side of the city. She married the minister of Calton Parish Church, and carrying out militant acts could not have been easy in her position. She and artist Ethel Moorhead were caught in an attempt to set fire to an empty mansion at 6 Park Gardens in July 1913, and were sentenced to eight months imprisonment.[1] She went on hunger strike repeatedly to secure release under the Cat and Mouse Act. After the Great War, she gave much valuable service in the venereal disease and child welfare clinics run by Glasgow Corporation.

The Glasgow suffragettes took militant action only reluctantly. It began with window smashing and pillar box attacks in 1912, escalating to arson and bombing of empty properties in 1913 in an effort to pressurise the government through the insurance companies. While the

Postcard of Anna Munro, Organiser of the Women's Freedom League in Scotland, 1908.

Mummy's a Suffragette.

A typical anti-suffrage postcard.

attempts to burn 6 Park Gardens, Shields Road Station and to bomb the Kibble Palace were unsuccessful, elsewhere, a considerable amount of damage was done. In April 1913 the Western Meeting Club at Ayr was burned to the ground, followed by attacks on the Royal Observatory in Edinburgh, and the Gatty Marine Laboratory and Leuchars Station in Fife. In December, 1913, Kelly House at Wemyss Bay was burned to the ground in a spectacular fire which was visible for miles along the Firth of Clyde.

Only one item from this militant period has survived, in the form of an Indian club, one of the many weapons confiscated by the police at the meeting in the St. Andrews Halls in March, 1914 which ended in a major riot. The Glasgow suffragettes were prepared for trouble — the flower-screened platform was protected by barbed wire, and personal weapons were carried — as Mrs. Pankhurst, released from prison on hunger strike, was to make an illegal appearance. She was smuggled into the hall in a laundry basket, but the meeting was brought to an abrupt halt when the police led a brutal baton charge against the platform.

Many of the suffrage souvenirs are attractive — screen-printed silk scarves in the suffrage colours of purple, green and white, banners, some of which were sewn at the Glasgow School of Art, pottery, and a variety of badges. There is also a complementary collection of anti-suffrage material, including propaganda postcards and a nasty little "Jenny-in-the-box" toy which pops up with a "Votes for Women" banner.[2]

The People's Palace also has a collection of photographs of Helen Crawfurd (1877-1954) a much-jailed militant suffragette who went on to lead the Glasgow Women's Peace Crusade during the First World War, and to help with the organisation of the 1916 Rent Strike, which forced Lloyd George to pass the Rent Restriction Act. She became a founder member of the Communist Party of Great Britain in 1921 and was also secretary of the Workers International Relief Organisation and involved with the International Co-operative Women's Guild. Her travels took her to Russia and Europe.[3]

The Co-operative Women's Guilds in Glasgow played a central role in the lives of many working class women until the 1950s. The first guild was established in Kinning Park in 1892, and the movement spread rapidly. It gave women the opportunity to get out of their homes, discuss political and other matters, and to socialise.[4] In recent years, with the demise of the Scottish Co-operative Wholesale Society and a changing social mileau, many of the guilds have ceased to operate, and their bannerettes, attractively stitched and painted, have come into the care of the museum.

The temperance movement also offered similar opportunities to women, and the once-familiar white enamel bows with the pendant stars of honour (awarded for recruiting other members) of the British Women's Temperance Association are now part of the museum collections. Rarer still is the little mother-of-pearl brooch in the form of a hatchet, sold as a souvenir of Carry Nation's (the "Original Bar Room Smasher" of the Ohio Whisky Wars) visit to Glasgow in 1908.

Often, the People's Palace collects information and artefacts relating to the history of ordinary Glasgow women. The Carry Nation hatchet brooch came with two portraits of the woman who bought it, Mary Carmichael, who with her husband ran the Crossburn Dairy in Cowcaddens. One is a wedding portrait of 1894; the other shows her in her working clothes, a red striped blouse and black apron which were the typical dairy workers' clothes of the time.

Another interesting, although anonymous portrait is that of a Glasgow woman shopkeeper of about 1790, possibly in Hutcheson Street. Every detail in the portrait is indicative of the wealth, prosperity and independence of the sitter — her gold earrings and buckle, her jet necklace, the range of goods in the shop which include lemons and a cannister of fine hyson tea, and the chest on the shelf which shows her to be a

Mary Carmichael of the Crossburn Dairy, Cowcaddens wearing her working clothes and photographed with her milk cans.

A Glasgow woman shopkeeper of the 1790s.

trustworthy person who could keep the property and records of a Friendly Society. Portraits of working women of independent means in the 18th century are rare; usually they are depicted in a family role as wife or daughter.

The women's history collection covers a wide range of subject matter and in date ranges from St. Thenew (mother of St. Mungo, patron saint of Glasgow) who lived in the sixth century to present day Glasgow writer Liz Lochhead, whose portrait was painted for the People's Palace in 1977 by Alasdair Gray.

Chapter

9
Leisure Time

The history of how Glaswegians have spent their leisure time is as vital and as important as that of their industry, enterprise and scientific discovery, although historians have not given the study of leisure the same serious attention. Looking at the material remains of the leisure industry — the theatre and cinema bills, programmes and architecture, the football, cycling and swimming memorabilia, the printed bills for soirées, "bursts" and concerts can be as instructive as it is pleasurable, for much can be learned from how people have found enjoyment and relief from their daily work.

Nevertheless, many pastimes have generated little or no material culture, or have left only the flimsiest pieces of ephemera. It is difficult for most of us, bred in a cinema and television culture, to imagine just how much entertainment was to be had simply by being out on the street. A penny song sheet of 1853, entitled "Saltmarket Street, Glasgow on a Saturday night" ("Third issue of 10,000 copies") gives an indication:

> In Saltmarket Street on a Saturday night
> Half of the people in Glasgow (or very near)
> 'Twixt six and twelve are walking there;
> All other streets are deserted quite
> For Saltmarket Street on a Saturday night.

The same writer found praise for Argyle Street in the same terms, but on a Sunday night:

> For humour, merriment, frolic and fun
> There's not another place under the sun
> That ever gave me so much delight
> As Argyle Street on a Sunday night
> There was niffers, drivers, giggers and bellers

Weavers, shavers, haircutters and curlers
Rich and poor, old and young
All to fill up the mirthful throng
Swells, scarce four feet in their boots,
Puffing away at penny cheroots
Cutting it fat with all their might
In Argyle Street on a Sunday night.

These literary gems came from the pen of the Poet's Box "the Grand Temple of the Muse! The boast and pride of Millions! The Attraction of Cities! The Glory of Nations! And the Luminary of the world. No. 6 St. Andrews Lane, off Gallowgate Street, and first street from the Cross, right hand side". While his collection of songs and stories were, according to his own claim "unparallelled in the pages of British history" he also made a living by selling "Laces for 1d. a dozen, soap for lovers bearing the lover's charm, 1d a cake; all youths who are now looking over the nest ought to have a cake; ink a penny a bottle; Bell's matches or large sliders, for a farthing a box. The Poet's blacking all admire, its beautiful gloss sheds a lustre no other Blacking can do; The price is only ½d. a packet".[1]

In spite of claiming to have "the only Poet's Box in the West of Scotland" there were at least half a dozen such "poets" plying their trade in Glasgow. James Lindsay of King Street claimed always to have 5000 ballads on hand, with "a great variety of Picture books, song books, Histories etc. Shops and hawkers supplied on liberal terms". His printing establishment at 28 Nelson Street and 56 Trongate seems to have been bigger than W.M. Leitch's Poet's Box. He advertised "Hand bills, Circulars, Invoices, Business and Fancy Cards, Large Posting Bills, Society articles, pamphlets and letter press printing of every description, neatly and expediously executed on modern terms".[2]

The ballad criers and hawkers who sold such songs and stories in the streets were regular customers of these publishers. Hawkie, alias William Cameron (d.1851), a beggar, street orator and wit, left a graphic description of ballad crying in Glasgow in his autobiography. Arriving in Glasgow with only three pence to his name one Saturday night in 1818, he bought a dozen ballads at two pence. Starting out at 6pm, he began to spin tales to anyone who would listen, gathered a crowd, and sold his ballads. He returned to the shop and bought another three dozen. He sold these quickly and kept returning to the shop for further supplies, and by the time the shop shut at 8pm, he had made six shillings.

Hawkie was recognised as one of the more successful "patterers", but had a jealous rival called James McIndoe (d.1837) alias "Jamie Blue". On one occasion they held a competition to see who could sell the most of a particular chapbook. Hawkie managed to sell fourteen shillings' worth, while Jamie Blue made only a shilling and fourpence in the same time. Although both were handicapped by a fondness for whisky, Jamie Blue had the additional disadvantage of being totally illiterate.[3]

Speech or ballad criers who found a successful or unusual "book" tried hard to protect it from the many others who were trying to survive in the same trade. Glasgow had so many cheap printers and flying stationers however, that a crier who could obtain a copy of the desired work could take it elsewhere to have it printed within hours. The small jobbing printers in Glasgow then seem to have been as efficient and as numerous as today's instant printers.

The cause of the popularity of news sheets, chapbooks and ballads was the relative expensiveness of the newspapers prior to the repeal of the Stamp Tax in 1855. Naturally the street criers increased at times of public executions, and Hawkie tells us that when a man was being hanged on 7th April, 1819 for theft and housebreaking, fifty criers were arrested and jailed for crying the news of the execution. Hawkie escaped detection as there were seven other criers using crutches like himself.

While street crying declined with the advent of cheap newspapers, an interesting and idiosyncratic twentieth century survivor of this genre was Alexander Wyllie Petrie, the Glasgow Clincher. Petrie was a hairdresser to trade, and had a sharp wit by virtue (according to his own claim) of having a silver cell in his brain. He wrote, printed, published and sold a small newspaper called "The Glasgow Clincher" which claimed to clinch any argument. The "Clincher" was first published in 1897, and sporadically until Petrie's death in 1937. Much of it was witty, and a great deal of it was scurrilous. He criticized the police, the army, and above all, Glasgow Corporation, unmercifully.

> "There is no man in Glasgow will make money if he has brain power. It is only imbeciles who can make money, creeping through the Foundry Boys and the YMCA. Mixing their religious lies with the Name above all names, they enter the Town Council and are quite safe. . . .[4]
>
> The bungling generals remind me of the fumbling businessmen in Glasgow. If an assistant comes to his work five minutes behind time he gets notice to leave, but should a bauch of a character half ruin the establishment, there is not a word said about it".[5]

Some of his opinions were considered dangerous and he was harassed continually by the police, who had him committed to Woodilee Lunatic Asylum. However, he managed to find two doctors who certified him as sane, and he was soon back in George Square, selling his newspaper and parading himself as "the only certified sane man in Glasgow". The incident gave him good copy for his columns and regular features included "Out on Bail" and "Woodilee Wanderings". Glasgow learned

84

Portrait of the Glasgow Clincher, painted shortly before his death.

to tolerate the Clincher, even when he applied for the post of Chief Constable, publicly promising to be "a terror to evildoers from the Lord Provost down to the most humble Corporation official". Portraits of him and copies of his newspaper survive in the People's Palace collections.

Itinerant ballad criers and the Glasgow Green orators could be heard throughout the year, but their numbers increased dramatically at the time of the Glasgow Fair. Since mediaeval times, the Fair has been held in mid July, at the time of the feast of Saints Peter and Paul. In the 18th century, the Fair was sited at the foot of Stockwell Street, the southern entry into the town, and from the beginning of the 19th century until 1870 was held on Glasgow Green opposite the High Court.

The Fair changed in character over the years, and many descriptions of it and ballads about it survive. From time to time, the Fair was the scene of riots, as in 1791 and in the 1820s, special constables were enrolled to control the activity. In 1840 however, the correspondent of the "Glasgow Herald" expressed the regret that the Fair was not so good as in days of old — the Giantess of 1840 was "not so noble, and coarser spoken" and there was no Punch and Judy.[6] Nevertheless, the Fair of 1840 was not lacking in attractions. Wombwell came to town with fifteen wagon loads of wild animals and an enormous carriage containing two elephants and a rhinocerous. Wombwell was a regular visitor to Glasgow, and some years previously, one of his lionesses had fulfilled the awesome prophecy of Alexander Peden — that the day would come when lions would be whelped on the Green of Glasgow — by giving birth to two cubs. The place of this wonderous event was still being pointed out, by those who remembered it, in the 1860s. In 1840 one could also see re-enactions of the eruption of Mount Vesuvius in two separate places — the Apollo Saloon opposite the jail, erected by Springthorpe for this and his mechanical waxwork figures, and at the Zoological Gardens, Cranstonhill, where Mr. D'Ernest, artist in fireworks, had set up in business.[7]

The theatrical magazines commented on other eruptions in 1840. John Henry Alexander, the flamboyant manager of the licensed or legitimate Theatre Royal was actively prosecuting a minor showman, David Prince Miller, who had erected the Sans Pareil Pavilion at the foot of Saltmarket and was staging what Alexander considered to be "drama". The licensed theatres at that time had a monopoly of drama. Miller was relatively new to Glasgow; he had first come to the Fair in 1839, but in 1840, his booth was a substantial wooden structure, capable of seating 1000-1200 at a penny a time, and obviously a threat to the Theatre Royal monopoly.[8] Miller's outfit could perform Shakespeare's Richard III twenty seven times in seven hours and in his opinion "we excelled in our art, for at any theatre in the kingdom it would occupy fully two hours and a half . . . whereas we could perform it in twenty minutes!"[9]

Every Glasgow Fair brought a rash of such booths with their blood and thunder dramas, burlettas and equestrian acts. Built of wood and canvas or even brick and sometimes on a grand scale like the Adelphi (1842) and the City Theatre (1845), they tended to be of a semi-permanent nature. In 1845, there was a movement to get rid of them after they were proclaimed a nuisance and encroachment on Glasgow Green. In September, 60,000 people signed a petition to get rid of the structures at the west end of the Green owned by Miller, Cooke and Anderson.

The most impressive of these was John Henry Anderson's City Theatre. Capable of seating 3000, it had a stage, side wings, scenery, orchestra, boxes, pit and gallery. Anderson, "The Wizard of the North" was determined to outshine his rivals. He took up residence in Monteith Row (No. 3 on map) among Glasgow's business and professional classes.[10] The success of his theatre was short lived however. It opened for the Fair of 1845 and was burned to the ground in a spectacular fire of 18th November that same year. The Adelphi suffered a similar fate in 1848. Nevertheless, the battle of the minor theatres was fought and won on Glasgow Green; by that time, the monopoly of the licensed theatres had been broken, paving the way for the development of the music hall and variety theatres.

The Glasgow Fair always had its darker side. J. F. S. Gordon, the Episcopalian minister of St. Andrews-by-the-Green Church was one of many who pressed to have it moved from Jail Square and Glasgow Green. He noted with satisfaction that in 1870, the shows and the public hangings were "almost similtaneously Gibbeted" when the former were moved to Vinegarhill. He described the Fair in the following terms:

"The Cantrips resorted to by the several "Proprietors" to attract Customers were clever and dexterous in their own way; but the deafening Shoutings and Clangour which issued from the manifold Comedians, Tragedians, Clowns, Drums, Brazen Trumpets and all kinds of Music, rendered the whole scene a shocking Babel. Jugglers, Thimble-riggers, Card-sharpers, and all the Tramps in the three Kingdoms looked forward to Glasgow Fair . . . handless Dolts who thronged in from the Mining District and Hamlets in the neighbourhood, risked their lives at the Shooting Tubes, the Guns being loaded with Ball. . . . The colouring Materials of the Edibles and Drinkables were Poisonous. I have seen a human Brute skin with his teeth 20 Rats in so many minutes. . . . Frequently, poor Creatures in the last stages of Consumption were upon hire, and were exhibited 150 times a day, for weeks, as "Living Skeletons". . . . Penny Theatres, half darkened, were crammed every half hour from 10 till 10 with unkempt Hizzies, with whom every filthy joke and Liberty were taken . . . every Philanthropist cannot but exult in

"THE BARRAS, 1984" by Avril Paton

the final annihilation of the Shows at the Glasgow Fair and laud *Sic transit gloria mundi*".[11]

The Shows were not annihilated by the move to Vinegarhill. Side shows of the type described by Gordon survived there, in the various wax-works in Glasgow, and indeed at the Barrows until relatively recent times. The childrens' shows with mechanised amusements and rides still visit Glasgow Green at the time of the Fair to this day.

One sport which has disappeared from the Green altogether is that of swimming. Peter Walsh, one of the Glasgow Green orators described the swimming during the 1840s and 50s as "an unforgettable sight. Both sides of the river was black with people — lying, sitting or standing in the warm sunshine — as they watched the men and boys diving, ducking and playing all sorts of fantastic tricks in the water".[12] One of these boys, Walter Freer, who later became manager of Glasgow Corporation Halls, remembered with delight diving from the spring-boards at the east end of the Low Green, while wondering why the swimmers did not die of disease from the filthy and polluted water.[13] The passion for swimming in Glasgow in the 1850s was similar to that for marathon running in the 1980s, and it was on this account that the public baths were built.

For most of the 19th century, the great spectator sport in Glasgow was the regatta. Throughout the summer, regattas were held every Saturday, attracting thousands along the length of the Clyde between Nelson's Monument and Rutherglen Bridge to cheer the different participants in the race. Once a year, a three day event was arranged which attracted competitors from all over Britain. Tents and marquees were erected on the Low Green, and there was a general carnival atmosphere.[14]

Football did not supplant the regatta as the major mass spectator sport in Glasgow until the early years of the 20th century. Glasgow Green was really the birthplace of Scottish football — both the Rangers (1873) and Celtic (1888) teams had their origins here. In the days before the Great War, supporting one's team was an almost ritual affair, with a procession of the brake club, with the team colours, banner and horse drawn brake marching to the ground and returning in a similar fashion after the match, the result being displayed in large letters on the side of the brake. Not many of these early brake club banners are known to survive, but the People's Palace is lucky to have the banner of the Vale of Clyde Brake Club (1900) among its collection of football memorabilia.

While the boxing booths were a feature on Glasgow Green, either at the Open Air Gymnasium (built 1860, near Humane Society House) or as part of the Glasgow Fair, the sport in the days before the introduction of the Marquis of Queensberry Rules in 1867 was clandestine, bloody

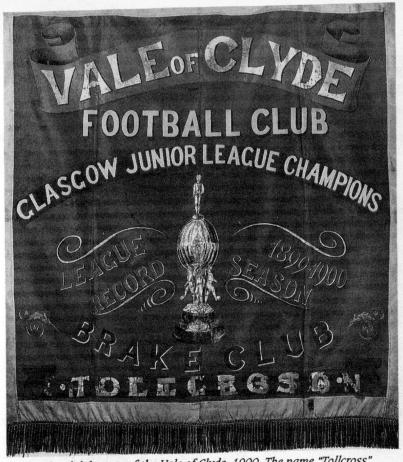

Brake Club banner of the Vale of Clyde, 1900. The name "Tollcross" has been painted over "Shettleston" indicating the club's movement.

and brutal. Bare fist fights were held in lonely deserted places — Eaglesham Moor, or fields near Dunoon or Falkirk — with no holds barred. There would be a mass exodus from Glasgow to witness the fight, with heavy betting on the result among those unable to attend.[15] Boxing later became a means whereby talented young men like Benny Lynch (1913-1946) could escape from their drab existence.[16] Gorbals-born Lynch, who became British, European and World Flyweight

Benny Lynch, the world-famous Glasgow boxer.

Champion, was a legend in his lifetime and there is a portrait of him in the People's Palace.

Some of the first moving pictures to be shown in Glasgow were of boxing matches. It is generally agreed that this new form of entertainment was introduced into Scotland at Christmas 1895 when pictures were shown at Glasgow's Barracks Carnival ground, Gallowgate, by George Green. For many years, moving pictures were shown in between music hall acts or turns or in the fairground and it was not until about 1910 that the cinema became an entertainment in its own right.[17] Eventually, it overtook the music halls in its popularity. In a similar fashion, the owners of the Metropole Theatre in 1948 secured for their performances "The Latest Sensation — Television!"[18] little realising that this wonder would ultimately be the death of both music hall and cinema.

The history of the thirty odd theatres and music halls which have flourished in Glasgow is a rich and complex one for which there is no space here. While thousands of bills and programmes have survived in various public collections to testify to the variety of the entertainment offered, special mention might be made of the colourful pictorial collection of bills for the pantomimes and shows at the Royal Princess Theatre c1900-1935 in the People's Palace collections. These were discovered during the demolition of the Palace Theatre in Main Street Gorbals in 1977. Under the management of Rich Waldon and Harry McKelvie, the Royal Princess produced annual pantomimes which ran

Poster for the 1924 pantomime at the Princes's Theatre in Gorbals.

"Private Towser", music hall artist, in 1899.

from December almost into the summer, and the popularity of which was due to the scenery, special effects, and above all, the topicality and locality of the book. "Simple Simon" of 1923 was set in a mythical Barlinnie Prison where prisoners were able to play golf and have all home comforts. "Hi Diddle Diddle" of 1924 featured "the Glasgow Subway of the Future" which had dining cars and space for dancing. Other items rescued from the Palace Theatre, designed by Bertie Crewe and first opened to the public in 1904, were some internal features and fittings including the pay box. The splendid plasterwork of the boxes which featured Nautch girls standing on elephant heads was given to the National Theatre Museum in London.

While much two dimensional material survives to illustrate theatre history, stage props and costumes are much rarer. However, one music hall turn — J. A. Wilson's performing poodle, "Private Towser" — survives stuffed, complete with collar and other props, in the People's Palace collections. Wilson, "The Black Oracle, the Greatest Negro Comedian" was one of the many blacked-up entertainers popular at the turn of the century, and he and his dog often topped the bill at the Good Templar concerts in the Bridgeton Temperance Institute and the Wellington Palace.

Naturally, the People's Palace attempts to cover popular entertainment and entertainers up to the present day, and its varied collections include a 1959 juke box and the 1974 stage clothes of Billy Connolly.

10
Public Art

Glasgow's tenement architecture brought about the evolution of a distinctive form of public art in the manner in which the common entrances or closes were decorated.

The closes were usually painted to dado height and whitewashed above. In the areas of the city where the factor or property manager had an interest in maintaining the standard of the property, the closes were whitewashed and painted on a regular basis and the costs shared by the tenants or owners. This is still the case.

To brighten the closes, different bands of colour paint, usually in contrasting dark colours were employed, and often, between the paint and the whitewash, a decorative band of stencilling was added. Fashion, cost effectiveness and loss of skill in doing stencil work have meant that the bright Victorian closes have been overpainted in two plain colours, but there are still some places in Glasgow where the original painted schemes can be seen.

The basic reason for keeping the closes freshly painted was a sanitary one. The Sanitary Department, established by Glasgow Corporation in 1870 and dedicated to eliminating typhus fever, ultimately had an effect on the decorative finishes of the closes. Tiles were considered to be more sanitary and easier kept than painted surfaces, and in an effort to avoid the sickening encrustations of filth which were all too common in the older slums like the infamous Factory Land (see page 60) builders began to tile closes to dado height.

In order to make the houses more attractive to prospective tenants and buyers, architects and builders chose decorative tiles for the dado band. In many cases, a band of stencilling was still added to the plaster above the tiles, often complementing them, and where the tiling stopped on the first landing, the different bands were echoed in the paintwork which continued. Only in the grander tenements was the tiling continued from the ground to the top floor.

*Tiles designed by J. Moyr Smith in the Queen's Arcade, Cowcaddens.
Demolished 1968.*

In many closes, the decorative tiling was not limited to the dado. Often panels depicting flowers or stylised plants were used at intervals along the full depth of the tiling. This type of close decoration was common in the red sandstone tenements of 1900-1914 done in the art nouveau style.

As a general rule, the most lavishly decorated closes are found in the grandest tenements. This is not always the case however. An elongated daffodil, growing through five tiles was rescued from a modest tenement of two-roomed houses in Craigmore Street in Parkhead in 1974. Similar tenements on Balgrayhill, Springburn, were decorated with picture tiles in blue and black, showing scenes from the Bible and designed by Glasgow-born artist John Moyr Smith.

Tiled or "wally" closes were always more desirable than plain painted closes. Although thousands of beautifully decorated tiled closes were lost in the era of comprehensive redevelopment 1955-1980, the housing associations which have assumed responsibility for tenement rehabilitation have since recognised the fondness of Glasgow people for wally closes, and have retained or replaced the tiles, and have even in some cases introduced tiles to the older closes. Inverse nostalgia found expression in the old pantomime song:

It's oh that I'm longing for my ain close
Nane o' your wallies — just a plain close

The washing of the common stair once a week by each of the residents in turn gave rise to a complementary but much more ephemeral art form, the chalking of the stair down either side with different patterns. These could be loops, lines or zig-zags or even chains of flowers executed in pipe clay, and lasting a week until the next resident washed the stair.[1] Blocks of pipe clay dissolved in water, with some disinfectant added was the traditional mixture for cleaning the stairs. These blocks were reproduced commercially by Glasgow's biggest clay pipe works — White's, Christie's and McDougalls — for that purpose in red and white, and the art form ceased when the last of the pipe works closed in 1968. At the present time, only one Glasgow firm still produces a stair wash mixture which imitates the effect of dissolved pipe clay, but the stair wash patterns have been forgotten by all except the older generation.

The appearance of tenement closes was also brightened by the addition of stained and painted glass to the windows of the common stair, and sometimes to the inner doors of each house. Such glass was produced in great quantity by many of the thirty or so stained glass studios in Glasgow — Guthrie & Wells, Meikle, Stephen Adam, and the City Glass Company to name but a few.[2] The subject matter was not always adventurous. Flowers, fruit, trees, birds, ships and the Four Seasons were commonly used, in different styles and combinations, and these added greatly to the attractiveness of the closes.

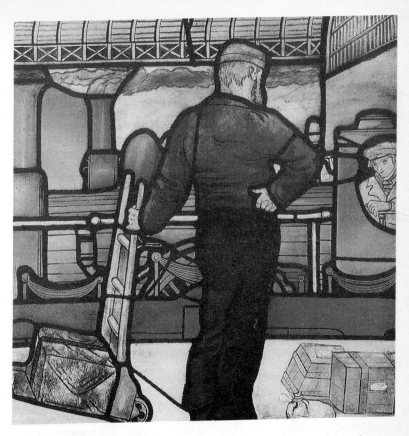

"The Railwayman". One of twenty panels designed by Stephen Adam for the Maryhill Burgh Halls, 1877.

Such was the bread and butter work of the stained glass studios. The artists and designers employed their greater creative talents in working on special commissions for churches, ocean-going liners, the big private houses of Glasgow's industrialists, and public buildings both at home and abroad. Between 1870 and 1914, Glasgow became one of the centres of excellence for the design and production of stained glass, and while much has been lost through demolition and redevelopment, a great deal remains as a testimony to Glasgow's pre-eminence in this field.

Because of redevelopment, much Glasgow glass has been rescued for the People's Palace collections. An interesting series of panels which may be mentioned here are the twenty executed for the Maryhill Burgh Halls in 1877 by Stephen Adam, showing the trades and industries of Maryhill, from boat-building to glass-blowing.

The architects of public halls and those engaged in the fitting of shops took full advantage of the sanitary and decorative properties afforded by tiling the walls. The St. Mungo Halls in Gorbals, built for the United Co-operative Baking Society in 1906 (demolished 1984) had a variety of different types of art nouveau tiles in its corridors. The Govan Burgh Halls, built 1901 (refitted 1975), had their corridors tiled to dado height in a refreshing green and yellow leaf pattern. In the Queen's Arcade in Cowcaddens (demolished 1968) shoppers were entertained by columns decorated in Moyr Smith tiles ranging in subject matter from fairy tales to trades and crafts.

Dairies, butchers and fish shops were also tiled for health reasons, but many shops incorporated appropriate picture panels at their entrance and continuous tiled friezes around the inside of the shop. In butchers' shops, cows and sheep grazing or going to market were common themes, while in fish shops, fishing boats, liners and mermaids featured prominently. There are picture panels from several shops in the People's Palace collections.

In order to meet the demand for tiles, there were 26 firms operating in Glasgow by 1900. The firm of James Duncan Ltd (1865-1966) was one of those specialising in the provision of picture panels, and the tiles were often manufactured to the requirements of the customer. The designs were drawn up in Glasgow and executed by the tile manufacturers in Staffordshire.[3]

Another Victorian feature of Glasgow shops which is rapidly disappearing with time is the shop sign — the gilded fish from the fishmongers', the giant spectacles from the opticians and the large copper top hat once common to the hatters. The People's Palace has some distinctive signs in its collection, including a pair of giant eyes from Pringle's, Opticians in Saltmarket, the model tramcar which sat above the Old Tramcar Vaults Pub and the Highlander from the HLI Bar (both Maryhill Road), a large gilded key from Henderson's Locksmiths in Gallowgate and a giant mortar and pestle (once lit by gas) from Trimble's Pharmacy in Dumbarton Road. The hanging shop sign was a relic from times when people were less literate and could understand a sign easier than the printed word. In the museum context these signs are symbolic of a way of life which has passed, and of the many once familiar Glasgow businesses which now no longer exist.

The closes, public buildings and halls decorated with tiles and glass, and sometimes fenced with stylish cast iron, the picture panels in the shops and the distinctive shop signs above, and the stained and leaded glass in the churches are but some of the features which can be considered as the contents of the most public of public art galleries — the street itself. While it is sad that many of these familiar and reassuring features should have to be removed from their original sites, it is better to have them in the museum than to see them disappear altogether. As part of the museum collection, they make the People's Palace the institution which Lord Rosebery hoped it would become — a palace of pleasure around which the people might place their affections, and which might give them a home on which their memory could rest.

While there are different art forms in which Glasgow excelled, the artists who chose to depict the city in the past are relatively few in number. The People's Palace has examples of the works of some of those who did, including panorama artist John Knox (1778-1845), watercolourist Andrew Donaldson (1790-1846) and his pupil Thomas

A primitive watercolour of Old Partick Bridge, c1870.

Pastor Jack Glass beside the Knox monument, by Alasdair Gray, 1977.

Fairbairn (1820-1884). Other artists represented include Andrew MacGeorge (1810-1891), Sam Bough (1822-1878), David Small (1846-1927) and William Simpson (1823-1899) all of whom were excellent topographical artists. The museum also has a small collection of drawings of Glasgow people by artist Harry Keir (1902-1977) who specialised in depicting working class life, and a series of etchings by Ian Fleming, depicting the city during the Second World War.

In 1977, the People's Palace was fortunate in obtaining the services of artist and writer Alasdair Gray who did a series of 30 works featuring Glaswegians in settings chosen by them, thus combining portraiture and topography. Red Clydesider Harry McShane was drawn beside the Weaver's Monument in the Old Calton Burying Ground, writer Alex Scott was painted in the Pewter Pot Pub and Pastor Jack Glass of the 20th Century Reformation Church chose to be painted beside the monument in the Necropolis dedicated to John Knox, leader of the 16th century Reformation.

Billy Connolly, 1983, with the portrait painted by John Byrne in 1973, in the People's Palace.

The museum has pursued a policy of acquiring modern works depicting both Glasgow and Glaswegians, and artists represented include Ernest Hood, Ken Currie and Alexander Guy. A major work is playwright John Byrne's eight foot high portrait of Billy Connolly, 1973.

The contemporary work being done by artists in Barlinnie Prison's Special Unit is also represented in the collections in the context of the prison artwork which has flourished from the time of the Napoleonic prisoners onwards. There are ceramic pieces by Bob Brodie, and a small sketch in sandstone for a head of Christ by Hugh Collins, done in preparation for a life size figure for St. Columba's Church which was unfortunately rejected by the congregation in 1984. The achievements of Barlinnie's Special Unit in terms of the art produced are remarkable, and it is fitting that this unique experiment in penal reform should be represented in the People's Palace.

Sketch for the controversial statue of Christ, by Hugh Collins, Barlinnie Special Unit.

Chapter

11
Religious Life

The full motto of the City of Glasgow is "Lord Let Glasgow Flourish by the Preaching of Thy Word and the Praising of Thy Name". A more secular society has shortened this to "Let Glasgow Flourish" but from the earliest times, the Christian religion has played a fundamentally important part in the social and political development of the city.

From mediaeval times, after the burgh charter was granted by King William the Lion to Bishop Jocelyn around the year 1175, the economic development of the town was also inextricably linked with the church. Glasgow was a bishop's burgh and the secular administration, the levying of tolls and taxes and the conduct of the Fair, was carried out by the bishop and his staff until the time of the Reformation.

Many people in Glasgow before the Reformation of 1560 must have depended indirectly upon the church for their livelihood, and there is no evidence to suggest that the reformed religion was introduced with the kind of image-smashing and destruction which took place elsewhere. Indeed, the survival of the Cathedral with its choir and part of its rood screen intact, and the traditional stories about the Incorporated Trades defending the Cathedral against attack by the Reformers indicates that the Reformation was perhaps not universally welcomed.

Nevertheless, very little has survived to represent the pre-Reformation church, with the exception of some of Archbishop Beaton's books, and odd manuscript fragments discovered in the bindings of later books.[1] The little altar statue of St. Eloi, patron saint of the Hammermen, discovered under the floor during the demolition of Rutherglen Parish Church in 1794 indicates some attempt to save religious items from destruction.

The change from Catholicism to the reformed religion did not mean that there was a separation between the religious and the secular. If anything, the relationship was stronger, and as the minutes of the Kirk Session show, the reformed church had control over the education and the morals of the people. The dedication of Glasgow people to their religion was always a cause for comment by English visitors. Spencer in 1771 for example remarked that: "The inhabitants have been remarkable for their strictness in attending to the public and private worship of God so that in going past their doors in an evening, you may hear so many singing psalms, that strangers are apt to think themselves in a church".[2]

At the same time, the Town Council took seriously its duty of keeping the various city churches in good repair and seeing that they were stocked with suitable communion plate. In 1704 for example, they commissioned goldsmith James Luke to make twelve silver communion cups;[3] one of these, inherited by Blackfriars Church, is now in the People's Palace collections.

There is no space here to deal with the complex history of the various ecclesiastical secessions and schisms which took place in the 18th century, but mention might be made of some. The Old Scotch Independents, who counted no less than David Dale among their members, were established in 1768. Some of their communion ware is in the People's Palace collections. The first Methodists came to Glasgow in the 1750s, and the first Methodist church was opened in 1779.[4]

The first religious body to meet in Glasgow which was not of Presbyterian persuasion was the Episcopal church. Episcopalians were recorded in Glasgow in 1715, and the first purpose-built Episcopal church to be erected in Scotland was St. Andrews-by-the-Green (No. 8 on map) in 1750. It attained notoriety when an organ was installed in 1775, and was thereafter known as "the whistling Kirk". It ceased to be a church in 1975, and some of its distinctive Gothic pews, its pulpit and its windows were removed to the People's Palace.

Catholicism was re-introduced into Glasgow in the 1790s, with immigration from the Highlands and Ireland. The first Catholic chapel was built in Marshall's Lane, Calton in 1797 and was the sole place of Catholic worship until St. Andrews Cathedral was built in Clyde Street in 1816.

The great expansion in church building in Glasgow happened after the Disruption of 1843, when those who disagreed over the question of patronage left the Church of Scotland to form the Free Church. In 1847, the United Presbyterian Church was formed by those who disagreed with the Free Church over the matter of state establishment. Three separate Presbyterian communions were therefore building churches simultaneously and sometimes in the same street, a situation which has caused conservation problems for a shrinking church population.

The United Presbyterian built the biggest and most grandiose buildings often with spires and usually lavishly decorated in the interior. A good example of U.P. architecture is Dowanhill Church, designed by the architect William Leiper with interior decoration and stained glass by

Daniel Cottier.[5] Capable of seating 1100 people its interior was meant to inspire, with its blue-painted ceiling studded with gold stars and its vibrant rich stencilling in reds, blues, greens, yellows and black, which earned it the nickname of "Dr. Baxter's ice cream parlour". A later congregation had the scheme painted out, but the great Gothic pulpit seat and collecting dishes, presented to the People's Palace when the congregation moved elsewhere have now been restored to their former glory as a testimony to the adventure of U.P. decoration.

FROM
Glasgow Tramcar to Gospel Platform.

The Testimony of Evangelist Seth Sykes.

Lantern slide from the life story of Glasgow evangelist Seth Sykes (1892-1951).

At the opposite end of the scale are the mission halls which had no architectural pretensions and which in some cases, were little more than wooden huts. Since the great evangelical revival campaigns by Moody and Sankey in the mid 1870s, the mission halls have been part of Glasgow's spiritual geography but like other churches have suffered from redevelopment and population movement. The largest of them — the Tent Hall, the Grove Institute and the Seamens' Bethel — have disappeared.

What the mission halls lacked in architecture was made up in spiritual fervour. Their informality, their warmth, their emphasis on born-again Christianity appealed to many working people who felt alienated by the established churches. A good instance of the type of work carried out in the mission halls is exemplified in the evangelical partnership of Seth and Bessie Sykes, who began their work in the streets of Springburn during the General Strike of 1926. Seth Sykes was a tram conductor with Glasgow Corporation, and the open air evening meetings which he and his wife Bessie organised were aimed at children. Songs were sung and games played, and the meetings were so popular that the community who attended them, poor although it was, clubbed together to buy Bessie a new American portable organ in 1927. This was gifted to the People's Palace after it had given over 50 years of service. Music was an important aspect of their work, and some of the Gospel choruses composed by them, such as "Running Over" and "Love Wonderful Love" became known and sung world wide.

Springburn was a railway community and the Sykes' family work was for some time centred on the little Railway Mission building in Vulcan Street, erected 1887 and demolished in 1983. By 1929, the couple were receiving so many requests for meetings, that Seth Sykes gave up his job to devote all of his time to evangelism, and from then until his death in 1951, the couple travelled the length and breadth of Britain in their work. They assembled a wonderful collection of lantern slides, and anyone attending a Sykes meeting would be assured of a feast of music and pictures. After her husband's death, Bessie Sykes carried on the work alone, until her own death in 1982.[6]

No branch of the Christian religion has been exempt from the contraction, closure and demolition of the last two decades. Even the great Catholic churches, such as St. John's in Portugal Street, Gorbals designed by Pugin and built only in 1896 have been cleared away, with immense loss of architectural wealth in the furniture, fittings and glass. The material loss is undoubtedly much greater than that at the time of the Reformation in 1560, and it is the purpose of the museum to record and rescue as much as is practicably possible.

Chapter

12
The Glasgow People

In a local history museum, the history of the people should always be a major consideration. Glasgow's ethnic background is varied and interesting. From the time of the 1745 Jacobite Rising, Glasgow has received, accommodated and absorbed wave after wave of immigrant people. The first immigrants were those driven from the Highlands, some by force, and some throughout the 19th and early 20th centuries by necessity, in search of work and better prospects. Community spirit among the Highlanders, as with other immigrant groups, was always very strong, and certain occupations were favoured by them. The sporting successes of Partick Police Force were in no small measure due to their strapping Highland constables. The decline of the Highland community spirit in recent years is symbolised by the closure (1978) of the famous Highlander's Institute in Berkeley Street, but the space under the Central Station railway bridge in Argyle Street is still known as the "Highlanders' Umbrella" from the days when poor Highland immigrants found shelter and solace in one another's company there.

With the decline of cottage industry and the coming of the industrial revolution, people from many rural parts of Scotland flocked to Glasgow in search of work. The difficulties and distress encountered by them were such that specialist societies were established to help them with money, work, and other necessities. The People's Palace has certificates for the Glasgow Ayrshire Society (established 1761) and the Glasgow Kilmarnock Society (1855). The Glasgow Angus and Mearns Benevolent (established 1838 to help the incoming people from that area) formally wound up its affairs in 1978 and the Presidents gold chain, snuff horn, gavel and other memorabilia, were presented to the People's Palace with the consent of the Queen Mother, Patron of the Society. There were dozens of other similar societies in Glasgow, dedicated to helping the casualties of a shifting population.

The biggest immigrant influx was that of the Irish. Made possible by the first Glasgow to Belfast steamboat which started in 1818, the movement accelerated with the demand for cheap labour to build canals, railways and bridges and with the economic disaster of the Great Irish Famine of 1845-50. The Irish brought their politics, culture, and religion with them.[1] By the turn of the present century, there were scores of branches of the Irish National Foresters and Hibernian orders all over Glasgow, and the museum has examples of their regalia. While the Hibernian pageants and marches ceased with the decline of the usefulness of the organisation as a Friendly Society, their Protestant counterpart, the Orange Order, has gone from strength to strength. Collecting historic Orange material has been slightly easier, and besides the usual sashes and ceramic figures of King Billy, the museum even has a flute, treasured for generations by a family who believed it to have been played at the Battle of the Boyne in 1690.

Sometimes this movement and assimilation of peoples can be symbolised in a single object. The museum has a marriage bottle of cheap brown glass, engraved for the wedding of L and M Gilmartin in 1881. The couple, who were both Irish, had emigrated to Glasgow in the late 1870s with their respective families, met and married. The bottle is engraved with the date, entwined hearts, Irish shamrock and the Glasgow coat of arms, and although poor at that time, they went on to establish a successful stevedoring business which lasted until the 1940s.

The acrimony between Irish Catholic and Protestant was not carried into Glasgow's commercial life. The clay pipe and pottery manufactories in the city for example made goods aimed at all political and religious shades of the Irish market. A price card for MacDougall's Clay Pipes survives in the museum collections, listing 168 pipes aimed at the Irish market alone, including Dublins, Derries, No Surrender, Wolfe Tone and Red Hand of Ulster pipes.

A much smaller, but equally distinctive immigrant group are the Glasgow Italians. They came from the poorer parts of Italy from the 1880s onwards, bringing with them a new style of catering. Many started with ice-cream or hot chestnut barrows on the streets — the People's Palace has the chestnut roaster on which the Crolla catering empire is founded — and graduated to cafes and fish restaurants.[2] While fish and chip shops were unknown in Italy, in Glasgow they were run almost exclusively by Italians, and the museum has a drawing by Harry Keir of one in Shamrock Street which claimed to be Glasgow's first. The brightly painted ice cream parlours and the willingness of the Italians to work on Sundays brought out the wrath of Glasgow's sabbatarians in the early years of the present century. The literature of the Sunday Traders Defence Association, some of which survives in the museum, is printed both in English and Italian.

The Glasgow Jewish community has also made a significant contribution to the life of the city. When the first synagogue was opened in

1823 there was only a handful of Jewish people, but their numbers were increased in the 1880s with the persecutions in Russia.[3] One of the many fields in which they shone was that of entertainment, and the People's Palace is lucky to have the large collection of bills and programmes from the historic Metropole (formerly the Scotia) Theatre in Stockwell Street, gifted by impressario Alex Frutin.

The entire history of Glasgow can be seen as a movement of its peoples, with the influx of immigrants on the one hand and the exodus of Glaswegians, sometimes in very great numbers, to all parts of the globe. The museum has a poster advertising a sailing for the first Scottish Colony in New Zealand (1839) and offering free passage to unmarried women.

In 1983, the City of Glasgow launched its "Welcome Home" celebrations to attract emigrants back to the city. To mark the event, Charles, Lord Forte (himself an Italian immigrant and now head of the great Forte hotel and catering empire) made a generous gift of silver ware to the city and the People's Palace. The pieces made were selected from a competition among students of the metal work department of the Glasgow School of Art, and the theme chosen was Glasgow's immigrant peoples. One of the pieces, designed by Richard Weaver in tryptych form, shows Glasgow's relationship to the rest of the world. The other, designed by Helen Marriot is in the form of a bowl, symbolising unity, with a ribbon of blue niobium, representing the Clyde, the way by which most of the immigrants arrived. Round the rim are engraved the different words for "home" in nine immigrant languages.

While the museum displays attempt to indicate something of the movement of Glasgow's population, much work goes on behind the scenes to record individual life histories. This is done through making tape recordings of or notes about Glaswegians who have experienced something which is part of a past way of life. For example, there are recordings of James B. Aird, who was raised in extreme poverty in the Gallowgate and survived the great influenza epidemic of 1919. His memories of Green's carnival, and Pickard's waxwork in Trongate have proved invaluable. David Gouk, who began his working life as a reel boy with Pathé Frèrez has recorded a life time's experience as a cinema distributor and his inside knowledge of the cinema industry in Glasgow. Cecilia Russell recorded her experiences as a pawnbroker's assistant and a suffragette in Glasgow before the First World War. Mrs. N. McKinlay recorded her work as a pot painter in the last days of the Britannia Pottery. These are but a few examples.

Many more members of the public regularly write down their experiences for the museum record. John Francey and Alex Knox for example have given notes on their experiences of the Barrows and Glasgow Green in the inter-war years. Mavis E. Thom sent from Canada notes about her father and his family before they emigrated from Glasgow's

Gorbals in 1906. Such notes and information, however brief, are always welcomed.

13
Glasgow Green Today

In the recent past, the Green had an atmosphere of its own. Alex Knox who was familiar with it in the 1930s describes it thus:

> "If it was a 'nice dryin' day' the ropes would be out on the drying greens forenenst the wash house, and what with the smell of freshly washed clothes, and the aroma of freshly baked bread wafting across the Green from the Co-operative Bakery in McNeil Street, aye, and the peculiar smell from Templeton's Carpet Factory, the Green in those days had a bouquet all of its own. . . . A great aroma came from the Camp Coffee works in Greendyke Street, and the smell of freshly roasted coffee fair titivated my nostrils".[1]

Today, with the loss of industry and manufacture the air is much more sterile, and while traditional livestock is no longer grazed on the Green, among the new attractions to be seen are the award-winning Clydesdale horses owned by Glasgow Parks Department.

While the older sports of golf and swimming have not been practised for some time, and while boxing is now unknown in the area, the marathon runners have embraced the Green as their own. The first Scottish People's Marathon was staged in the autumn of 1982, and the organisers mapped out the 26 mile route beginning at the Saltmarket and finishing on Glasgow Green, outside the gates of the People's Palace. The large flat areas of the Green afford ample space for assembly in advance of the marathon, and room for the refreshment, medical treatment and family reunion areas at the end of the race. The avenue of mature trees in the Green carriageway provides a superb setting for the last few hundred yards of the race, while the People's Palace makes a splendid backdrop for the presentation of the prizes.

Marathon running is truly a people's sport, for it needs no specialist or expensive equipment and anyone can participate. It has become exceedingly popular in Glasgow, and the Scottish People's Marathon, with over 15,500 entrants per year is the third largest marathon event in the world. It is appropriate that it should begin and end on the people's park.

A similarly appropriate development is the staging of the Glasgow International Folk Festival on the Green. In 1984 the first tented village was erected on the Green, and singers and dancers came from all over the world to perform there. Free dance performances were given to the thousands assembled in the grounds of the People's Palace, the winter gardens being too hot in the scorching sun but readily available in case of rain. Folk groups now perform in the winter gardens throughout the year, while Glasgow Green has become the home of the Folk Festival.

Mention has been made of the part played by folk song in preserving the rights of the Green in the past, and it is likely that with the revived interest in the Green by the sporting and folk community, all detrimental encroachment (including the motorway plans which have been deferred but not quashed) will be firmly opposed in the future.

In the late 1970s, the future of the People's Palace was in question because of the amount of repair work required to be done to the building. The institution found Friends however, who with the local community councils and other bodies were anxious to see the building preserved and promoted, and after much hard work, its future has been secured for the next generation. Folk singer Alastair McDonald in his "Songs of Scotland" series has recorded a song by A. Jamieson which, because it is one of the few songs in the world to be written about a museum, and because it summarises so well the feelings of the people of Glasgow towards their Palace, is produced here, by way of conclusion, in full.

THE PEOPLE'S PALACE

As I went walkin' wi' the weans
And my wee wifie Alice
I telt a stranger I'd just met
About my eastern palace
Says he tae me "That just can't be
You're not a King Old Bean"
But I proved him wrang
With the words o' a sang
On a place called the Glesca Green

Chorus   Come alang wi' me if you want to see
The Palace o' the People
Standin' alone in the red sandstone
Wi' a big high dome and steeple.
The place vibrates wi' the Glesga Greats
For the workin' man they spoke
Be you grave or gallus, take a trip to the Palace
It belangs to the Glesga folk.

There were galleries great in the year '98
In the west end o' the city
Kelvingrove was a treasure trove
But there just remained one pity
'Twas a horse drawn tram or a walk wi' a pram
Till the day that they were released
Frae the hassle and the malice, by the building o' a Palace
For the folk that were broke in the east.

Now you'll learn o' Glesga if you seek
How Gaelic the Dear Green Place is
We've a coat of arms that's quite unique
Our history proudly traces.
St. Mungo is the Patron Saint, depicted you can see him
All this and more you will find in store
In the old P. P. museum.

So come wi' me and we'll go and see
This winter garden treasure
And lets spare a thought for yon fine lot
Who fought to save our pleasure
Let's never take for granted this old structure fair & fine
It's standin' there for us all to share
For the Palace is yours and mine![2]

Postscript

Over the last ten years, the fortunes of the People's Palace as a Glasgow institution have undergone dramatic changes. In 1976-7, when the GEAR (Glasgow Eastern Area Renewal) initiative was announced by the Scottish Development Agency, museum staff, in partnership with the Partick Camera Club, made a full record of the Calton district prior to the great changes which were to take place.

The discovery of dry rot in the museum building in 1978 seemed symptomatic of the decaying east end of Glasgow. The winter gardens had been closed since 1966 after a Parks Department decision to demolish them, because of the high maintenance costs and low visitor figures. The gardens were opened briefly for the 80th birthday celebrations of the People's Palace in 1978 and closed again when a report revealed that the decaying structure was highly dangerous.

A report for GEAR on the listed buildings of the east end in 1979, which was still current in 1983, gave the People's Palace an estimated life of five years "or less if the Fire Department decide to close it down". It was at this point that the Friends of the People's Palace were formed with the express purpose of saving the building, campaigning for adequate visitor facilities and a return to the Victorian values of the Glasgow Corporation members who originally intended to have a People's Palace in every district of Glasgow.

In 1981, in spite of an award-winning exhibition on Glasgow stained glass, the building, isolated by the new building works in Monteith Row and deprived of a host population by the GEAR redevelopment, reached an all time low with a mere 80,000 visitors. With the gardens closed, large parts of the museum closed for dry rot eradication, and a major mains collapse in the driveway outside, the future of the People's Palace looked bleak.

Fortunately, the will and the money were found to restore the fabric completely. The history of the building and its collections caught the imagination of film makers, and a string of films, both on the People's Palace and using its collections, brought the museum to a wider public. Increased use of the Green brought more visitors. The Glasgow Folk Festival adopted the Green as its main site, and in 1986, after an absence of decades, the Glasgow Trades Council brought the annual May Day March back to the Green.

The first full length film on the People's Palace was screened in 1983 and the visitor figures began to rise. A healthy 202,000 was recorded in 1984, increasing to 254,000 in 1985, 308,000 in 1986 and 407,000 in 1987. With all parts of the building completely open from March 1987 for the first time in decades, visitors continue to flock to the building. The winter gardens is a popular venue for evening parties, concerts and wedding receptions.

The Friends of the People's Palace have done much to publicise the building. In 1986, they commissioned Margery Clinton, one of the foremost ceramic artists in Scotland to make a porcelain replica of Smudge, the cat employed by the Parks Department. The story of Smudge has been featured in countless newspapers and magazines, and the profits from the sale of the cats has been used to promote the People's Palace.

The increase in visitors has been outstripped only by the growth of the collections. These have been increased to approximately six times the size they were in 1975, when a specific acquisitions policy was pursued actively for the first time. While every aspect of the social history collections has been enriched, some collections have been built from scratch; the 200 panels of Glasgow stained glass have been collected since 1978 and the temperance collection of several hundred items was created through public appeals in 1979.

The People's Palace has never attempted to function as a traditional art gallery but the value of art within social history, topography and popular culture has not been ignored. Acquisitions have been made because of the Glasgow content of the piece in question, and there are no esoteric objets d'art in the collection. Norman Kirkham's large vibrant portrait of "Fran and Anna", Peter Howson's "City Bar", Avril Paton's huge "Barras" painting all have immediate meaning for the Glasgow visitor. Some pieces are amusing, like Graeme Gilmore's 1986 "Glasgow Punk Rocker" with his mohican hair cut of twelve inch spikes and his pram chassis which makes him a visual and witty pun. Other pieces have a practical use, like George Wyllie's "All-British Slap and Tickle Machine" which offers the visitor a bit of slap and tickle, and does a robust public relations job for the People's Palace when it goes out on loan. Some pieces, like Valerie Pragnell's "Tenement Summary" (a peeling window frame, with broken jagged glass and torn lace curtain arranged in the dark days of comprehensive redevelopment, before Glasgow became Miles Better) can encapsulate an entire era.

For some years, annual commemorative exhibitions have been held in the museum with a view to attracting a wider and different audience, and to building up or strengthening different aspects of the collections. The bicentenary commemoration of the Calton Weavers in 1987 was viewed as an important landmark for the history of the Scottish labour movement, but with the prospect of acquiring 1787 objects being small, a different approach was taken. The great empty dome, 25 feet above the museum's temporary exhibition gallery on the top floor was selected as an area for a commemorative and permanent mural on the subject of 200 years of labour history.

The artist who accepted the challenge of filling this space was Ken Currie, whose Glasgow School of Art Diploma work was acquired by the People's Palace in 1983 because of its draughtsmanship and his willingness to interpret contemporary issues of fundamental importance, such as War and Peace. He undertook the commission with vigour and imagination, painting a great history panorama which puts the small, often insignificant objects

117

in the museums collection into context, giving them meaning. Much of the history of the ordinary people survives in documents, in word-pictures only, and as far as Glasgow is concerned, few artists have attempted to paint these subjects. Ken Currie has been the first to represent on canvas the struggle of the Calton Weavers, the planting of the Liberty trees, the great Reform Bill processions, the foundation of the trades unions, the introduction of scientific socialism, the teaching of John Maclean, the hunger marches of the Thirties, the Upper Clyde Shipbuilders' work-in of the Seventies, and the May Day processions of today, all within a Glasgow context. While academic historians might not value such exercises, the works are important for those with an interest in modern history who wish to see such subjects examined and re-interpreted in comprehensible terms. The Glasgow history mural was the largest local authority commission since the Banqueting Hall murals in the City Chambers at the end of the 19th century, and Ken Currie has been hailed by art critics throughout Britian as one of the most talented artists working in Scotland in the 1980s.

The earlier centuries of Glasgow history present even more problems of interpretation. Until the time of the Reformation, Glasgow was a flourishing bishop's burgh, relying on the cathedral shrine and ecclesiastical administration for its wealth. On account of the thoroughness of the Reformation, few artefacts remain as witness to the period. A handful of broken stones, keys to buildings long since demolished, and small pieces sifted from archaeology sites are in themselves inadequate objects with which to interpret several centuries.

A policy of re-interpretation was adopted with regard to existing objects. For example, the recumbent effigy of Robert Wishart, Bishop of Glasgow 1271-1316 survives in Glasgow Cathedral, minus head, feet, hands, crozier and attributes. Wishart was a figure of national and international importance because of his support of William Wallace and King Robert Bruce during the Wars of Independence against the English, both in practical terms (putting the cathedral resources at the king's disposal) and at the Papal Court. A cast of his damaged effigy had been in the museum collections since 1900, and was not in as good condition as the original in the Cathedral. In 1985, a sculptor from the School of Art, having studied similar effigies elsewhere, "replaced" all of the parts missing since the Reformation of 1560 and painted the cast. Other original fragments of the Wishart tomb were identified in Paisley Abbey, and cast for the restored effigy, to give as complete a re-interpretation as possible.

With the change of use and demolition of so many Glasgow churches of all denominations, it is possible that the material destruction of the period 1955-1985 will be recognised by generations to come as having been even more physically damaging than the period 1555-1585. Recognising the parallel through coping with the consequences (the rescue of stained glass, church furniture and other artefacts from Glasgow churches) museum staff will re-use neo-Gothic Victorian artefacts to interpret the mediaeval history of the city.

Because of the expansion of the collections, and the new-found popularity of the museum, it has long been recognised that extensions to the building are required. A fire escape and lift are also necessary, as well as more display space and better visitor facilities. In the years leading up to 1990, both the museum and winter gardens seem likely to be turned into building sites again, as the necessary work is undertaken, and it is hoped that visitors will be patient a little longer.

In the summer of 1987, Glasgow District Council announced plans to redevelop Glasgow Green. These were precipitated by the ravages of Dutch Elm disease, which will decimate the trees on the Green, and the Garden Festival, which after its closure may afford some opportunities of re-planting the Green. The proposed plans involve £55 million redevelopment money and include the following: the construction of a five star hotel on the edge of the Green, the removal of all Clelland's carriageways, the removal of the weir to enable pleasure boats to ply a longer stretch of the Clyde, a waterway bisecting Flesher's Haugh to provide a circuit for them, a large artificial lake at the back of the People's Palace including a jet of water twice the height of Nelson's Monument which will cause a fine spray to play on the winter gardens. Traffic will be banned with the exception of a tram; sports and activities will be moved to beyond the periphery of the Green.

The very suggestion of such fundamental changes brought forth a torrent of criticism and unfavourable comment. The proposed changes were announced during the Glasgow Folk Festival of 1987 and Adam McNaughtan immediately took up the pen in defence of the Green:

> Come a' ye folk o' Glasgow, help to stop this new fiasco;
> They're gonnae change the Green holus-bolus,
> Wi' sluices, ponds and dams, an' trains and boats and trams—
> Everything except the breedin' gondolas.
> I'm willing to concede that some change is whit we need;
> The only thing I cannae thole is,
> They scheme schemes at the tap an' then jist tell us whit's to happen
> Withoot askin' whit the people want.

Chorus
> Now Glasgow Green's the heart o' the city that it's part o'
> But frae the map the Cooncil wants it aff,
> So they've gi'ed it to the planners an' this time they've went bananas
> Sayin', "We'll flood it for a laugh",
> To them it disnae matter if the Green is under watter—
> That's a typical planner's joke,
> But we want consultation before any alteration,
> 'Cause the Green belongs to Glasgow's folk.

Glasgow author Carl MacDougall pointed out that if this kind of redevelopment was suggested for Bannockburn or Culloden, there would be an outcry, and mindful of past struggles to protect the Green, many people see the proposed developments in terms of destruction rather than improvement. Time will tell.

Elspeth King.

Sources

Chapter 1

[1] *Glasgow Herald* 24th January, 1898.

[2] *Glasgow Weekly Herald* 13th December, 1879.

[3] For a complete account of municipal progress see *Municipal Enterprises Glasgow* (handbook issued by Glasgow Corporation for the 22nd Congress of the Sanitary Institute) Glasgow, 1904 and *Municipal Glasgow, its Evolution and Enterprise* (Corporation of Glasgow) 1914.

[4] *Municipal Glasgow* (1914) 3-4.

[5] Aspinwall, Bernard "Glasgow Trams and American politics 1894-1914" in *Scottish Historical Review* (1977) 64-84.

[6] *Municipal Glasgow* (1914) 2-8.

[7] Crawford, Robert *The People's Palace of the Arts for the City of Glasgow* (Ruskin Society, 1891).

[8] *The People's Palace for East London* (London, 1887).

[9] *The Palace Journal* vol 1 (1887) p43.

[10] *The Builder* 26th March, 1898.

[11] *Glasgow Herald* 24th January, 1898, see also Murphy, Wms. *Captains of Industry* (1901) 193-194.

[12] See typescript on the People's Palace in the Murray Collection, (Special Collections) Glasgow University Library; see also *The Bailie* 25th November, 1896.

[13] *Building Industries* 5th June, 1898.

[14] *Glasgow Herald,* 24th January, 1898; see also *The Bailie* 15th December, 1897 and 26th January, 1898.

[15] Programme for the People's Palace music hall, 1894, People's Palace collections.

[16] Limited Company Papers for the Glasgow People's Palace Company Limited. (Scottish Record Office) Ref. BT2/2782.

[17] *Glasgow Evening News* 20th January, 1898.

Chapter 2

[1] Quoted in Macphail, I.M.M. *History of Scotland* (2, 1958) 99.

[2] Sung on LP record, *Words Words Words* (1983). Trivial Fond label.

[3] McLellan, Duncan *Glasgow Public Parks* (1894) 23-25.

[4] For a full account of the improvements, see James Cleland's *Report respecting the Improvements in the Green of Glasgow with an Account of its Minerals,* Glasgow, 1828.

[5] Gordon, J. F. S. *Glasghu Facies* (1872) vol 1 605-607.

[6] Cleland, James *Enumeration of the Inhabitants of the City of Glasgow for the Government Census of 1831* (Glasgow, 1832) 255-256.

[7] Gordon op cit vol 1 545.

[8] Cleland *Report* (1828) p4.

[9] Gordon op cit vol 1 593-594.

[10] Ibid vol 1 402-405.

[11] Reports of the Glasgow United Evangelical Association, 1875-80.

[12] *Glasgow Mercury* 13th July, 28th September, 1790.

[13] *Glasgow Evening Citizen* 8th April, 1911.

[14] Records of the Glasgow Humane Society, Strathclyde Regional Archives, Ref. TD 249/1.

Chapter 3

1 Paton, James "A People's Palace", *Museums Association Annual Report* 1898.

2 Cowan, James *From Glasgow's Treasure Chest* (1951) 260-262.

3 Cleland, op cit (1828) 5-33, 19.

4 "Airn John" 12th June, 1858 in the Poet's Box collection, Mitchell Library.

5 Ibid "The Diggings in Glasgow Green" 3rd April, 1858.

6 Finlay, J. B., *Professor John Anderson and his Theatre* (1967). Illustrated London News vol 7, 1845 p349; see also Marwick, J. D. *Report by the Town Clerk as to the Common Lands of the City and Royal Burgh of Glasgow and specially as to Glasgow Green* (1891) 17-24.

7 *Glasgow Herald* 17th November, 1848.

8 Gordon op cit vol 1 600-601.

9 From the L.P. Words, Words, Words, (1983) on the Trivial Fond label.

10 Scottish Burgh Record Society. *Records of the Burgh of Glasgow* (1874) 21st June, 1576, p51-52.

11 *Glasgow Herald,* 30th April, 1858.

12 Logue, Kenneth J. *Popular Disturbances in Scotland 1780-1815* (1979) 155-160.

13 Gordon op cit vol 2, 768-769.

14 Berresford, Ellis P & MacA'Ghobhain, S. *The Scottish Insurrection of 1820* (1970).

15 See the James Moir Papers, Mitchell Library, MS204.

16 See Broadsheet, "Full account of the destruction of the Wooden Bridge", Special Collections, Glasgow University Library, Ref. Bh 14 x-5. *Glasgow Courier* 24th April, 1821.

17 *Glasgow Herald,* 8th September, 1884.

18 See McShane, Harry, *No Mean Fighter* (1978) 12-14, 17, 20-21 and Walsh P. *Glasgow Entertainments During the Last Fifty Years* (nd. c1930) 11-12.

19 *Glasgow Weekly Herald* 18th February, 1905.

20 King, Elspeth, *Scotland Sober and Free — the temperance movement,* 1829-1979 (1979) 7-9.

21 *Glasgow Green and Roundabout, A Tourist Guide* (1982) 22-23.

22 Minutes of Glasgow Corporation, Parks Committee, 1891.

23 Gordon op cit vol 1, 592-593.

24 Caldwell, John T. "The Battle for Glasgow Green" in *Scottish Labour History Society Journal* No. 16 (1981) 19-27.

Chapter 4

[1] Honeyman, T. J. *Art and Audacity* (1971) 63-64.
[2] See *Glasgow Herald* 14th December, 1912, 25th January, 1913.
[3] See for example *Glasgow Herald* 24th March, 1978.
[4] Murray, James "Stringhalt" *Runs with the Lanarkshire and Renfrewshire Fox Hounds* (1874).
[5] See Findlay, J. B. *Juggling Through four Reigns* (1945).

Chapter 5

[1] See Devine, T. M. *The Tobacco Lords* (1975). Nichol, Norman, *Glasgow and the Tobacco Lords* (1973).
[2] Thomson, Rev. James *History of St. Andrew's Parish Church* Glasgow (1905) 15-16.
[3] This unique clock is still owned by James Finlay and Company, Merchants of Glasgow.
[4] Oral information from the Lean family.
[5] See "A day at the Barrowfield Dye Works" in the *Penny Magazine* 1844.
[6] Fleming, Arnold J. *Scottish Pottery* (1923). This is still the standard reference book.
[7] Oral information, given at a Scottish Pottery Society meeting, 1973.
[8] Hume, John R. *Industrial Archaeology of Glasgow* (1974) 65.
[9] See *Macfarlane's Architectural Ironwork* (Glasgow n3d c1914) by Walter Macfarlane & Co., Saracen Foundry, Glasgow.
[10] Glasgow Post Office Directories.

Chapter 6

[1] Strathesk, John (editor) *Hawkie, The Autobiography of a Gangrel* (1888) 102-106.
[2] See Laidlaw, Stuart I. *Glasgow Common Lodging Houses and the People Living in Them* (1956).
[3] Municipal Enterprises — Glasgow 1904 (op cit) p67.
[4] The literature on ticketed houses is large and includes Dr. J. B. Russell's *Life in One Room* (1888) and *The Ticketed Houses of Glasgow* (Glasgow Philosophical Society lecture 1888); Peter Fyfe's *The Housing of the Labouring Classes* (1899) and *Backlands and their Inhabitants* (1901); William Bolitho's *Cancer of Empire* (1924).
[5] King, Elspeth "Peter Fyfe, Photographer" in *Cencrastus* No. 14 (1983).

Chapter 7

[1] *Glasgow Courier* 10th April, 1821.
[2] See *The Trial of the Glasgow Cotton Spinners on Charges of Murder* (Glasgow 1838).
[3] Phillips, Alastair *Glasgow Herald* (1983) 23-25.
[4] Gillespie, Sarah C. *The Record of the Scottish Typographical Association 1853-1952.* (1953) 24-26.
[5] *Glasgow Herald* 8th September, 1884; see also *Quiz* 12th September, 1884.
[6] Marwick, W. H. *The Life of Alexander Campbell* (nd c1960).
[7] The firm of R. Paterson was established in 1849 and produced Camp Coffee in Charlotte Street until 1981. Most of the manufacture has since moved elsewhere.
[8] See Haddow, William Martin, *My Seventy Years* (1943) 55-56.
[9] Eds. Roberton, Sir Hugh and Kenneth *Orpheus with His Lute — A Glasgow Orpheus Choir Anthology* (1963).
[10] The standard works on John Maclean are John Broom's *John Maclean* (1973) and Nan Milton's *John Maclean* (1973).
[11] The standard work on Maxton are still Gilbert McAllister's *James Maxton, the Portrait of a Rebel* (1935), and J. McNair's *James Maxton: the beloved rebel* (1955).

Chapter 8

1 *Glasgow Herald* 25th July, 16th October, 1913.
2 For a history of women's suffrage in Scotland and catalogue list of the People's Palace collection, see Elspeth King's *Scottish Women's Suffrage Movement* (1978); see also the *Papers of the Glasgow and West of Scotland Association for Women's Suffrage* (EP Microform 1980) with introduction by Elspeth King.
3 Knox, William (ed) *Scottish Labour Leaders 1918-1939* (1984) 81-86.
4 Buchan, A. *A History of the Scottish Co-operative Women's Guild 1892-1913* (1913).

Chapter 9

1 Poet's Box collection, Glasgow Room, Mitchell Library.
2 Murray Collection (Mu 23 1-y) in the Special Collections, Glasgow University Library.
3 Strathesk, John *Hawkie, The Autobiography of a Gangrel* (1888) 90-97.
4 *The Glasgow Clincher* 16th February, 1902.
5 Ibid No. 26 vol 3.
6 *Glasgow Herald* 16th July, 1840.
7 Ibid.
8 Answers for John Henry Alexander . . . to the Bill of Advocation and Suspension at the instance of David Prince Miller, 23rd December, 1841. Special Collections, Glasgow University Library. Mu 24-b20.
9 Miller, David Prince *Life of a Showman to which is added managerial struggles* (1849) 111-112.
10 Ibid 122-127; see also *John Henry Alexander of the Glasgow Theatre Royal Versus John Henry Anderson of the Minor Theatre* (Glasgow 1842).
11 Gordon op cit vol 1, 580-581.
12 Walsh, Peter *Glasgow Entertainments During the Last Fifty Years* (nd c1930) 9-10.
13 Freer, Walter *My Life and Memories* (1929) 72-73.
14 Ibid 70-71.
15 See broadsheets on individual fights, Ref. Bh 15-x5, Mu 1-X11 in Special Collections, Glasgow University Library.
16 See Burrowes, John *Benny, the life and times of a fighting legend* (1982).
17 Scottish Film Council *Fifty Years at the Pictures* (1947) 3-6.
18 Bills in the People's Palace collections.

Chapter 10

[1] Barrapatter tape 2, People's Palace oral collection.
[2] See Donnelly, Michael *Glasgow Stained Glass* (1981) for a study of the history of stained glass production.
[3] Oral information from the Duncan family.

Chapter 11

[1] Dell, Richard "Some Fragments of Mediaeval Mss. in Glasgow City Archives" *Innes Review* (1967) 112-117.
[2] Quoted in Macphail, I.M.M. *History of Scotland* Vol. II (1958) 64.
[3] Scottish Burgh Record Society. *Extracts from the Records of the Burgh of Glasgow 1691-1717* (1908) 30th June, 1704 p382.
[4] Cleland, James *Rise and Progress of the City of Glasgow* (1820) 16-20. For the Independents, see McLaren, David J. *David Dale of New Lanark* (1983) 91-101.
[5] Dickie, Rev. William *History of Dowanhill Church 1823-1923* (1926) 70-95.
[6] See Sykes, Bessie and S. *A Great Little Man* (memorial volume for Seth Sykes 1952).

Chapter 12

[1] See Handley, James E. *The Irish in Scotland* (1947).
[2] Valuable oral work on the Irish, Italian and Jewish communities in Glasgow has been done in recent years and is published in *Odyssey* (2 volumes 1982) edited by Billy Kay.
[3] Gorbals Fair Society *A Scottish Schetl — The Jewish Community in Gorbals* (1984).

Chapter 13

[1] Knox, Alex *Reminiscences of Glasgow Green* People's Palace General notes 7/9.
[2] Song written by Alec Jamieson. Available on Corban Records, 1984.

John Glassford impersonated for the benefit of school parties, by People's Palace Education Officer Harry Barton.

WHAT PEOPLE HAVE SAID ABOUT THE PEOPLE'S PALACE

"The only museum of Glasgow in Glasgow." Dr. John Shaw, Scottish Oral History Newsletter.

"The city's premier museum of local history." Freddie Anderson in "Cencrastus".

"The People's Palace is real folk art . . . more people should come and see it." Betty McAllister, Scotswoman of the Year in the "Evening Times".

"We have absolutely nothing like it in Wales." Neil Kinnock, M.P.

"There is the People's Palace and there are other museums in Glasgow." Robin Ward in the "Spirit of Glasgow".

"A social history museum of quite unusual quality." Kenneth Hudson, Administrator European Museum of the Year Award and author of the "Good Museums Guide".